Contents

***

Illustrations

***

Dick Turpin (*Weidenfeld Archive*)

Modern Corsican bandits (*Weidenfeld Archive*)

The bandolero (*Weidenfeld Archive*)

Salvatore Giuliano (*Keystone Press/Hulton Getty*)

Lampião, the great bandit-hero of Brazil (*Editora Gráfica/Weidenfeld Archive*)

Still from the Brazilian film *O Cangaçeiro* (1953) (*National Film Archive*)

Giorgios Volanis (*Institute of Balkan Studies*)

Constantine Garefis, with his band (*Institute of Balkan Studies*)

Sandor Rósza, the great Hungarian brigand-guerilla (*Hungarian National Museum*)

Scene from Miklos Jancso's film *The Round-Up* (*National Film Archive*)

Execution of Namoa pirates

A Pindari (*Weidenfeld Archive*)

BANDITS

* * *

ERIC HOBSBAWM

ABACUS

First published in Great Britain in 1969
This new edition first published in Great Britain by
Weidenfeld & Nicolson in 2000
First published in paperback by Abacus in 2001
Reprinted 2003, 2004, 2007

A CIP catalogue record for this book
is available from the British Library.

ISBN 978-0-349-11302-9

Papers used by Abacus are natural, recyclable products made from
wood grown in sustainable forests and certified in accordance with
the rules of the Forest Stewardship Council.

Printed and bound in Great Britain by
Clays Ltd, St Ives plc
Paper supplied by Hellefoss AS, Norway

Abacus
An imprint of
Little, Brown Book Group
100 Victoria Embankment
London EC4Y 0DY

An Hachette Livre UK Company

www.littlebrown.co.uk

Preface

* * *

Some time in the early 1950s the present author became struck by the curious fact that exactly the same stories and myths were told about certain types of bandits as bringers of justice and social redistributors all over Europe; indeed, as became increasingly clear, all over the globe. Following Dr Samuel Johnson's injunction to

> let observation with extensive view
> survey mankind from China to Peru,

readers of this book will find them in both countries, and indeed in all inhabited continents. This discovery formed the basis of an essay, 'The Social Bandit', the first chapter of a book of studies in archaic forms of social movement, *Primitive Rebels* (Manchester, 1959). Ten years later, on the basis of further studies, especially in Latin America, this was expanded into the first edition of the present book (*Bandits*, London, 1969). This, in effect, formed the starting-point of the rapidly growing contemporary study of bandit history, much of which (certainly since Anton Blok's critique in 1971) has not accepted the 'social banditry' thesis, at least in its original form. Subsequent editions (for Penguin Books, 1971) and for an American publisher (Pantheon Books, 1981), both now out of print, revised and expanded the original text and took account of the mass of new material and those criticisms which seemed to me to be well-taken. What lies before the reader now is thus the fourth revised edition of *Bandits*.

There are three major reasons for preparing it, apart from the fact that various publishers still think that the book has not lost its interest. First, and most obviously, a number of the major works on the history of banditry have appeared since 1981, for instance on Chinese, Ottoman Turkish and Balkan bandits, on Latin America, the Mediterranean and a number of more out-of-the-way regions, not forgetting Friedrich Katz's long-awaited biography of Pancho Villa. These have not merely added new material, but greatly widened the way in which we can think of banditry in society. In the present edition I have done my best to take account of these new findings. (On the other hand, the critique of the argument of *Bandits* remains more or less where it was.)

Second, the rapid disintegration of state power and administration in many parts of the world, and the notable decline of the ability of even strong and developed states to maintain the level of 'law and order' they developed in the nineteenth and twentieth centuries, are once again familiarizing readers with the sort of historical conditions in which endemic, and sometimes epidemic, banditry can exist. In the light of contemporary Chechnya we read the Mediterranean bandit explosion of the late sixteenth century differently from the way we did in the 1960s.

The third reason is that the author himself, while proud of being the founding father of an entire branch of history, cannot avoid trying to answer the question suggested by a good historian's review of two books on banditry ten years ago: 'Not much of Hobsbawm's thesis still stands undamaged.'[1] If this really were true, there would be no case for a new edition of *Bandits*. It would simply be out of date and beyond salvation by mere correction and revision, though perhaps worth reading as a document of its time. In my view, this is not the case with *Bandits*. The chief criticisms of the original thesis are surveyed in part I of the Postscript to this edition, which modifies and expands the Postscript included in the 1981 edition.

Nevertheless, thirty years after its first publication, it is clear that both the argument and the structure of the book require some substantial rethinking as well as updating. I have tried to do this here, primarily by placing banditry, including social banditry, more systematically into the political framework – of lords and states, of the structures and strategies of both – in which it operates. Though this dimension of the subject is present in earlier editions of the book, I have now tried more clearly than before to see 'the . . . *political* history of the role of banditry . . . (as) central'.[2]

I have also taken account of the most cogent criticism raised against my book, namely my use of bandit song and story both to trace the nature of the social bandit *myth* and, rather tentatively, to see 'how far bandits live up the social role they have been assigned in the drama of peasant life'. It is now clear that they cannot be reasonably used for the second purpose at all. In any case the identifiable men around whom such myths formed, were in real life often very unlike their public image; including many of those cited as 'good bandits' in the early versions of this book. It is also now clear that they cannot be used for the first purpose, without a full prior analysis of this genre of literary composition, the transforma-tions of its public, its traditions, topoi, modes of production, reproduction and distribution. In short, balladry, like the tapes of oral history, is a very slippery source, and, like oral tradition, it is contaminated by the way in which it is passed through the generations. Nevertheless, it can and must still be used for certain purposes. I hope I have (this time) not gone beyond the bounds of common sense in doing so.

This is therefore a substantially extended and revised

edition, although the text of the original nine chapters, and of the Appendix, 'Women and Banditry' (now Appendix A), while modified where necessary, has not needed to be substantially rewritten. The major additions to the last (1971) British edition are the following: (1) an introductory 'Portrait of a Bandit' (originally published as the bulk of the Preface to the 1981 American edition); (2) a new chapter entitled 'Bandits, States and Power'; (3) an Appendix B, 'The Bandit Tradition' and a two-part 'Postscript' (modified and extended from the 1981 edition) which – as mentioned above – deals with the criticisms of my work and also surveys the survival of activities embodying the classical bandit tradition in the later twentieth century. The section on 'Further Reading' has been rewritten. The prefaces to earlier editions have been omitted.

By way of acknowledgement I need only repeat what I said in the original edition. Most of this book rests on published material, and on information extracted, or more likely volunteered with enthusiasm, by friends and colleagues aware of my interest in the subject, and seminars in various countries which criticized the arguments of the book and put me in the way of further sources. My debts to the growing body of bandit historiography are acknowledged with pleasure and satisfaction, all the more genuine since so much of this literature since 1969 is based on primary research stimulated by the first edition of *Bandits*. My own direct contact with the subject-matter of the book has been limited. Chapter 9 is based on several weeks' intensive research in 1960 into the career of Catalan anarchist outlaws, which I could not have undertaken without the help of, and introductions provided by, M. Antoine Tellez of Paris. The basic argument of Chapter 4 was confirmed by a day in the company of Don José Avalos of Pampa Grande, province of Chaco, Argentina, farmer and formerly sergeant of the rural police. In 1981, following a conference on bandits and outlaws in Sicily, I had the opportunity to meet two former members of the band of Salvatore Giuliano and others with direct knowledge of his activities. However, I owe more to several friends and colleagues in Colombia, Italy and Mexico with considerably more extensive first-hand contacts with the world of armed outlaws. I owe much to Pino Arlacchi and, for Colombia, to Carlos Miguel Ortiz, Eduardo Pizarro and Rocío Londoño and her friends, some now dead. My debt to the work of Gonzalo Sanchez and Donny Meertens should be obvious from the text.

London, June 1999   E. J. Hobsbawm

Portrait of a Bandit

**

The best way to enter the complicated subject of 'social banditry' which is the subject of this book is through the career of a social bandit. Here is such a case. It was compiled by an unknown student at the University of Addis Ababa, Ethiopia, whose paper was made available to me by his teacher. At the time I received this paper, based on local informants and periodical sources in English and Tigriña, I was not given the name of the author, for reasons connected with the uncertain political state of Ethiopia and Eritrea at the time. If he should chance to see this edition, and wishes to make himself known, I should be more than happy to acknowledge my debt to him.

Here, then, in a rather summary form, is the story of Weldegabriel, oldest of the Mesazgi brothers (1902/3–1964). Let it speak for itself.

In the days when Eritrea was an Italian colony, Weldegabriel's father, a peasant of the village of Beraquit in the district of Mereta Sebene, died in prison, where he had been put as one of the village representatives who opposed the appointment of a new district governor because he was not a native of the district. The widow blamed the unpopular governor, and called for blood-vengeance, but her sons were too young, local opinion was divided about the governor's guilt, and in any case the Italians banned blood-feuds. Her four sons grew up and settled peacefully as farmers.

Weldegabriel joined the colonial troops as an *askari*, served the Italians in Libya during the Italo-Ethiopian War of 1935–6 with two of his brothers, and in the occupation of Ethiopia (1936–41). After the British won they went home to farm again, with some cash savings, a little Italian, and a good knowledge of weapons and military skills. Weldegabriel was a good soldier, promoted to noncommissioned officer.

The Italian colonial order had broken down and the British were temporarily administering the territory. In the disturbed post-war conditions banditry flourished, the large body of disbanded *askari* forming a natural reservoir of potential recruits. Jobs were scarce and Eritreans continued to suffer discrimination as against the Italians. Immigrant Ethiopians had even fewer chances. Ethnic groups raided one another in the highlands in competition for land and cattle. Blood-feuds revived, since the Italian administration no longer stood in the way of the performance of this sacred duty. Moreover, in such conditions banditry seemed to provide reasonable career prospects, at least for a time. The Mesazgi brothers entered it via their old family feud, though the hardships of civilian life may have encouraged them to take this quarrel up again.

As it happened the district governor, son of the man who might have been held responsible for their father's death, made himself unpopular for much the same reason as his father, by appointing to village office a member of a minority clan settled in Beraquit village, but strangers by origin. Weldegabriel was jailed for opposing him on behalf of the village and, liberated after a year, further threatened. The brothers decided to kill the new governor – this was legitimate under the feuding laws – and for this purpose divorced their wives so that the police would not punish them, incidentally regaining by this means the mobility without which outlaws cannot operate. They shot him and went into a nearby forest, relying on friends and relatives for supplies. The majority of the village supported them as champions of village rights, but they could not in any case have offended their former neighbours by robbing them.

The minority clan, as well as the governor's kin, naturally opposed them and helped the British authorities. The Mesazgis avoided massacring them but tried, with fair success, to make life impossible for them locally. Most of them left and the brothers gained further local popularity since the land of the emigrants was now available for other villagers. However, the rest of the district considered them as ordinary bandits, because there was doubt about the legitimacy of the blood-feud. They were tolerated because they took care not to harm the local people who left them alone.

Since they needed wider support, not least to harass the governor's family, the brothers took to going round the villages urging the peasants not to work the plots of land assigned to the governor, and to share them out. By a mixture of persuasion and suitably judged strong-arm tactics they convinced various villages to denounce these semi-feudal rights and thus brought to an end the lords' right to land and free labour in the district of Mereta Sebene. At this point they came to be regarded not as plain bandits but as 'special' or social bandits. They therefore enjoyed protection against the police, who were sent to the area against them – at the expense of the villagers.

As the police cut them off from their sources of supply, the brothers had to go robbing along the regional main road. They were joined by other bandits. But since robbing fellow-Eritreans could lead to new feuds, they preferred to rob Italians. One of the brothers was killed, and the remaining two therefore took to killing any Italian for vengeance, thus acquiring a reputation as champions of the Eritreans. Though they probably killed no more than eleven, their feats were exaggerated by local opinion, which credited them with the usual heroic attributes and invulnerability of the social bandit. They acquired a myth. What is more, since the roads became unsafe for Italian drivers, Eritreans who had previously not been allowed to drive by the Italian administration or the British, were authorized to do so. This was welcomed as a rise in status and for the jobs which now became available. Many people said: 'Long live the sons of Mesazgi. They enabled us to drive cars.' The brothers had entered politics.

At this point (1948) Eritrean politics were complicated by the uncertainty about the future of the ex-colony. Champions of unity with Ethiopia opposed supporters of various formulas for eventual Eritrean independence. Prominent Unionists approached the bandits for support, and almost all Christian ones accepted because it gave them a sense of identity and security against the predominantly Moslem independence men. However, while the brothers supported the union, as sensible men they did not kill Eritreans for political reasons in order to avoid feuds, nor did Weldegabriel burn houses or crops. Support from Ethiopia gave the bandits not only arms and money but refuge across the border. However, while Weldegabriel took his share in terrorizing Eritrea into federation with Ethiopia and fighting the Moslems, he was careful not to involve himself or his home district of Mereta Sebena in fights which did not concern it directly.

When the UN had finally voted for federation the bandits lost the support of the Unionists and the Ethiopian government. Most of them were amnestied in 1951, but Weldegabriel held out until 1952, and was one of the fourteen bandits considered too infamous by the British to be allowed to stay in Eritrea. The British therefore arranged for these to be given asylum in Ethiopia, where they received some land from the Emperor in Tigré province and a monthly stipend from him. Alas, they were strangers now themselves and the local peasants were hostile. The Emperor's promise of less troublesome land, better allowances and free education for their children never materialized. All of the bandits except Weldegabriel drifted back to Eritrea.

He himself could have returned to Beraquit, since he was a respected member of the community once he ceased to become an outlaw. He had remarried his wife, since she was no longer at risk nor he forced to rove. The kin of the dead governor, his enemies, were still powerful in Mereta Sebene, and he and his family were still 'in blood' with them. So he preferred to live out his life in Tigré. He died at the age of sixty-one in a hospital in Addis Ababa. A commemoration service was held for him in Beraquit. As an Eritrean newspaper reported, it was attended by many Eritrean notables, and funeral singers sang songs praising his achievements. Eritrean patriots are in two minds about the career of Weldegabriel: a people's bandit, but one who was instrumental in making their country into a part of Ethiopia. But his politics were not those of the twentieth century. They were the ancient politics of Robin Hood faced with the Sheriff of Nottingham.

Western readers in the third millennium of their chronology may find the career of men such as the sons of Mesazgi strange and difficult to understand. The chapters which follow will, I hope, help to explain it.

1

***

Bandits, States and Power

He made them call him 'Lord'
Those traitors in his band,
His betters he despised:
He wanted to be *more* . . .

You, the low and unarmed people,
stick to fields and clods of soil,
leave off carrying those pistols:
digging is what suits you best . . .
Back you go to rural labours . . .
Don't disturb the world again.
Ballad on the death of the bandit Giacomo del Gallo, 1610[1]

On mountain and in forest bands of men outside the range of law and authority (traditionally females are rare), violent and armed, impose their will by extortion, robbery or otherwise on their victims. In doing so, banditry simultaneously challenges the economic, social and political order by challenging those who hold or lay claim to power, law and the control of resources. That is the historic significance of banditry in societies with class divisions and states. 'Social banditry', which is the subject of this book, is an aspect of this challenge.

Banditry as a specific phenomenon cannot therefore exist outside socio-economic and political orders which can be so challenged. For instance – and this, as we shall see, is important – in stateless societies where 'law' takes the form of blood-feud (or negotiated settlement between the kin of offenders and the kin of victims), those who kill are not outlaws but, as it were, belligerents. They only become outlaws, and punishable as such, where they are judged by a criterion of public law and order which is not theirs.*

Most country people since the development of farming, metallurgy, cities and writing (e.g. bureaucracy) have lived in societies in which they see themselves as separate as a collective group from, and inferior to, the group of the rich and/or powerful, though often, as individuals, dependent on one or other of them. Resentment is implicit in this relationship. As the verse of the city poetaster demonstrates, banditry makes this potential rejection of inferiority explicit, at least in the world of men. By its very existence it implies a challenge to the social order. Nevertheless, before the rise of the modern capitalist economy, social and economic relationships change only slowly, if they change at all. Almost certainly the ballad about Giacomo del Gallo would have meant much the same to listeners in Bologna at any time from the eighth to the eighteenth century, even though, as we shall see, he would probably not have been known as 'bandit' before the sixteenth century.[2]

Socially speaking, the history of banditry therefore falls into three parts: its birth, as pre-bandit societies come to form part of class and state societies, its transformations since the

---

* The novella *The Two Drovers* by Walter Scott illustrates this conflict of laws perfectly. On the road to the cities of the South a cattle-drover from the Scottish Highlands has a dispute about pasture with an English drover. The Englishman knocks down the Scot, who kills him, since by his standards the insult can only be avenged in this way. The (English) judge who tries the Scot for murder tells the jury that, by his own law, the accused is not a criminal, but a man carrying out his duty. Nevertheless, under the law of the United Kingdom they have no choice but to convict him as though he were a criminal.

rise of capitalism, local and global, and its long career under states and social regimes in between. The first, which seems in some ways historically the most remote, is really not so, because banditry as a mass phenomenon can appear not only when non-class societies resist the rise or imposition of class societies, but when traditional rural class societies resist the advance of other rural (e.g. settled farming against nomadic or transhumant pastoralists), or urban, or foreign class societies, states or regimes. In fact, as we shall see, historically banditry as an expression of such collective resistance has been very common, all the more so as, in these circumstances, it enjoys considerable support from all of the elements in its traditional society, even its holders of power. This is what links the semi-nomadic economy of clan herdsmen, who traditionally supplied the major source of bandits in the Balkans and Anatolia,[3] the free gauchos of the nineteenth-century Argentine plains resisting the city and bourgeois property laws jointly with their rural chieftains, and the twentieth-century Colombian coffee-growers protecting 'their' bandits. All resist the encroaching power of outside authority and capital.[4]

Apart from this special situation, banditry as a social phenomenon in the long second phase of its history, is about class, wealth and power in peasant societies. As the Sardinian Antonio Gramsci described the situation in his own island in the early twentieth century, 'the class struggle is mixed up with brigandage, blackmail, arson of woodlands, the maiming of livestock, the kidnapping of women and children, attacks on municipal offices'.[5] Insofar as it survives into an era of fully developed capitalism in the countryside, as we shall see, it expresses, more than anything else (except perhaps dislike of a remote government) a hatred of those who lend money and link farmers to the wider market.

There is, however, a major difference between the

banditry of the first two phases and the third phase. It is hunger. In the nineteenth- and twentieth- century regions of capitalist agriculture where banditry is to be found – the USA, Argentina and Australia come to mind – people in the countryside no longer faced death by starvation. In most of the classic bandit regions of the medieval and early modern centuries, e.g. around the Mediterranean, they constantly lived on the edge of famine. 'The rhythm of hunger determined the basic structure of the rhythm of brigandage.'[6] The great age of the Brazilian *cangaço* begins with the murderous drought of 1877–8 and reached its quantitative peak with that of 1919.[7] Or, as the old Chinese saying had it: 'It is better to break the law than to starve to death.'[8] Poor regions were bandit regions. The months of the farming year when food was scarce and not much farm-work was to be done, were the season for robbing. When floods destroyed the grain, they multiplied brigands.

However, what interests the social and economic historian is primarily the structure of banditry, social or otherwise, rather than the effects of bandits' activities on the wider history of events in their times. And indeed, most of the bandits who have become genuinely famous figures in song and story, are persons of purely local range and horizons. Their names and the details of their exploits hardly matter. Indeed, for the bandit myth, the reality of their existence may be secondary. Few, even among archive-rats, really care about identifying the original Robin Hood, if there was such a one. We know that Joaquin Murieta of California is a literary invention; nevertheless he is part of the structural study of banditry as a social phenomenon.

Politically the history of banditry is considerably more dramatic. What happened counts – sometimes very significantly. Kings and emperors have started their lives as bandit chiefs like – I am told – the Emperor Tewodros (Theodore)

II who ruled Ethiopia in 1855–8, or the warlord Chang-Tsolin (Zhang-Zuolin) who governed Manchuria between the collapse of the Chinese Empire and the Japanese conquest. For that matter, it has been not implausibly argued that the founder of Uruguay as a republic independent of both Argentina and Brazil, Jose Antonio Artigas, began his career as a bandit, or rather as a professional rustler and smuggler, which is not all that different.[9] Moreover, the history of banditry is largely the history of its occasional mass explosions – the transformation of a condition modestly endemic in many geographical environments into massive epidemics, or even – as has been argued for China in the 1930s – a pandemic. Indeed, the serious modern history of banditry probably begins with Fernand Braudel's discovery (in his great book on the Mediterranean) of the extraordinary pan-Mediterranean explosion of banditry in the last decades of the sixteenth century and the first of the seventeenth.[10]

This is because the history of *power*, that is to say of the capacity to establish control over people and resources by coercion, was subject to far greater variety and mutability than the slow-changing structures of the economic and social order.

To understand banditry and its history we must therefore see it in the context of the history of power, i.e. of the control by governments or other power centres (in the countryside mostly lords of land and cattle) of what goes on in the territories and among the populations over which they claim control. Such control is always limited to particular territories and populations, since up to the present all states or power-claimants, even the most powerful empires, have always had to coexist with others outside their scope. Moreover, even within their claimed range, for most of history power was limited in three ways: because the means of control available to authorities were inadequate for their purpose, because their adequacy depends to some extent on the willingness of subjects to obey and their ability to avoid obeying, and because (partly for this reason) authorities tried to control only some parts of their subjects' lives directly. Even today, for instance, the government of Colombia cannot control several areas within its territory except by periodic military incursions, and the Royal Ulster Constabulary knows that within some strongly Catholic districts of Belfast, de facto policing is conducted not by the state but by 'Republican' strong-arm squads.

Bandits, by definition, resist obedience, are outside the range of power, are potential exercisers of power themselves, and therefore potential rebels. Indeed the original (Italian) meaning of *bandito* is a man 'placed outside the law' for whatever reasons, though it is not surprising that outlaws easily became robbers. 'Brigands' were originally merely members of armed groups not belonging to some regular force. (The modern sense appears from the end of the fifteenth century.) 'Bandoleros', the usual Castilian term for bandits, was derived from the Catalan term for armed partisans in the unrest and civil conflicts which swept through Catalonia from the fifteen to the seventeenth century 'and in due course degenerated into banditry'.[11] *Celalis* was the term for the sixteenth- and seventeenth-century bandits in the Ottoman Empire who, a recent study has argued, served to reinforce rather than undermine the sultan's power; yet their name derives from the ideological (heterodox Islamic) rebellion of Seyh Celal in 1519, which led the government 'to use the label to justify its repression of bandits, even where these did not have any of the rebellious content or viability of the original *celali*'.[12] The *shiftas* of the Horn of Africa are, I am told, defined by a well-known Amharic dictionary as bandits who, having renounced the authority of king or emperor, live in forests or the wilderness, cause disturbances and refuse to pay taxes or tribute; in short, as robber-rebels. And, in traditional China at least, the potential link between banditry and the periodically expected overthrow of dynasties, was a commonplace of political thinking.

The history of banditry, including social banditry, cannot therefore be understood or properly studied except as part of the history of political power, which, at its highest levels, is the power of empires and states. In class societies before the era of modern capitalism, the power of, in the last analysis, physical coercion was also the primary foundation of economic power. That is to say, the main mechanism for appropriating the surplus wealth generated by those who actually produced it – overwhelmingly from the land – was force or the threat of force.[13] This is so no longer, although political power, i.e. the possibility of physical coercion, remains the foundation of the revenue extracted by states from the inhabitants of their territories. Refusal to pay taxes is punishable by law and refusal to obey the law, in the last analysis, by jail.

For most of the history of agricultural society, the political power under which the communities of ordinary countrymen lived under normal circumstances was local or regional. They lived under lords, with or without the asset of kin loyalty or supernatural backing, who could mobilize men and build up systems of force and patronage. Kingdoms or empires, where they existed, were occasional visitors rather than permanent residents, even where king or emperor succeeded in replacing, or at least supplementing, local law by their own state-wide law and judges as in medieval England and (among its Sunni Muslim subjects) the Ottoman Empire. Indeed, for the most part such power as king or emperor had, other than his power as a large patron and lord himself, operated through the agency of local and locally rooted patrons, who responded to negotiation more than to command.

The strength of lords and states was great, but intermittent. Their weakness was that they lacked the material means, including the forces of coercion and law, to keep *constant* control over all their populations – even the unarmed part – or any effective control over the more inaccessible parts of their territories. This applied even to local men of power, who were closer to their land and people than remote princes; in any case, in a world of many lords and family rivalries, there was usually some room for evasion. The very institution of formalized outlawry, from which bandits take their name, indicates the shallowness of the power system. *Everybody* was entitled to kill the outlaw, because no authority was in a position to apply their law to him.

If we look at states, the contrast is particularly striking. In the past two-and-a-half centuries the power to exercise physical control has been increasingly concentrated in the so-called territorial state or 'national state', claiming and, through the apparatus of state functionaries or those licensed by the state, exercising a virtually complete monopoly of power over everything that goes on within its borders. The central state apparatus reaches down directly to every single person on the national territory and, in democracies at least, every adult citizen, having the right to vote, reaches up directly to national government by electing it. Its powers are immense – far greater, even in liberal democracies, than those of the greatest and most despotic empires before the eighteenth century. Indeed this concentration of power in the modern territorial state is what eventually eliminated rural banditry, endemic or epidemic. At the end of the twentieth century it looks as though this situation might be coming to an end, and the consequences of this regression of state power cannot yet be foreseen.

We tend to forget that before the nineteenth century no state with a territory larger than could be walked across in a day or two, possessed sufficient knowledge, regularly updated, of who lived on its territory, was born and died there. None could even identify individuals outside, or even – as Natalie Davis's study of the case of 'Martin Guerre' suggests – inside their homes.[14] No state, before the railways, and the telegraphs, ancestors of the modern communications revolution, could know what happened in its remoter corners or move its agents rapidly to take action. Hardly any state before the nineteenth century could pretend to control its borders, or tried to, or indeed had clearly demarcated frontier-lines. No state before the nineteenth century had the ability to maintain an effective rural police force acting as the direct agent of the central government and covering its entire territory. Indeed, outside the Ottoman Empire no European state before the seventeenth century had the power to maintain a permanent national army, directly recruited, paid and administered by the central government. Moreover, much as kings and princes would have liked to confine the possession and use of arms to their own servants, it was beyond their power. In settled feudal societies the peasants had been largely disarmed – the situation in unsettled and frontier zones was rather different – but not the nobility and gentry. Only in the nineteenth century did the effective state monopoly of arms become possible, and indeed effective Western governments, with some notable exceptions like the USA, aimed to remove them almost completely from unofficial life, even of the aristocracy – and what is more, succeeded, at any rate until the 1970s.

Before the triumph of the modern national state, power

was therefore limited by the central rulers' inability effectively to monopolize armaments, by their inability to maintain in constant being and supply a sufficiently large and
effective body of armed and civil servants, and, of course, by
the technical inadequacy of information, communication
and transport. In any case, even in the most formidable
kingdoms and empires the physical force, whether of rulers
or lesser lords or even – as Kurosawa's great film *The Seven
Samurai* shows – of village communities trying to defend
themselves, depended on a supply of fighting men who could
be mobilized in cases of special need, and a supply of such
men who were more or less permanently available. Conversely, the political power was measured by the number of
fighting men a chieftain could regularly mobilize.

The weakness of power contained the potential for
banditry. Indeed, even the strongest empires – the Chinese,
the ancient Roman Empire in its heyday[15] – regarded some
degree of banditry as normal, and thought of it as endemic in
pastoral borderlands and other suitable areas. However,
where the structure of power was stable, the bulk of potential
bandits, unless they lived beyond its range, tended to attach
themselves to those who could reward them: as retainers or
hired killers and enforcers to lords, as soldiers, guards or
policemen to states. Banditry as a mass phenomenon, that is
to say independent action by groups of the men of violence
and arms, occurred only where power was unstable, absent,
or had broken down. Those were the situations when
banditry became epidemic, even pandemic as in China at
some times between the fall of the Empire and the victory of
the Communists. At such times freelance chieftains of armed
men could enter the world of real power themselves, as clans
of nomad riders and raiders by land or sea had once become
the conquerors of kingdoms and empires. And, of course,
even those who had no great social, political or ideological

ambitions, had far greater opportunities for robbery than at other times. The era of seventeenth-century wars in Germany, like the era of the French revolutionary wars, was the golden age of the robber bands (see below, p. 107). With the decline, or even the break-up and dissolution, of state power which we are witnessing at the end of the twentieth century, it is possible that large parts of the world are re-entering another such era.

Nevertheless, in the past five hundred years of bandit history power has rarely been absent or unstructured for so long that the leaders of autonomous armed groups have seen themselves as major independent actors on the political and social scene. They were rarely strong enough for that. Whatever their own ideas or aims, they had to be political realists. Their best chance was to maintain a degree of autonomy and, without ever committing themselves completely to any side, bargain with those prepared to pay the highest price for their support – i.e. those who could not achieve their ends without it. But in the last analysis they had to come to terms with whatever centres of superior power were prepared to tolerate them, or go under.

Hence the constant negotiations between empire and independent armed groups or communities in the Ottoman Empire, the highland fighters who could be resisters against the state or its agents, or both at the same time. Hence, during the Second World War, the failure of British emissaries to bring about a rising against the German and Italian occupiers among the free, and guaranteed non-Communist, martial clans of highland Albania. They were told (by Winston Churchill's son-in-law) that if they did not, Albania's future after the war would inevitably be in the hands of the Communist resistance movement, but though they had nothing against fighting anyone, they were not convinced. The proposal to put the clan future at risk by closing all its political options except one clearly made no sense in their world. As we shall see (below, pp. 115–16), a similar conflict of strategies and tactics ended the symbiosis of bandits and Communists in the Chinese Revolution. For the bandits, the Communists were only one of several possible allies or temporary patrons. They were in practice no different from warlords or the Japanese, though in theory perhaps closer than the others to the ideology of the great bandit novel of Imperial China, the *Shui Hu Zhuan*. For the Communists a sentimental attachment to the tradition of bandit rebellion, and even the young Red Army's extensive reliance on bandit recruits, could not conceal the fact that in the long run national and social liberation were not to be won that way.

So how does the social element in banditry, which champions the weak against the strong, the poor against the rich, the seekers for justice against the rule of the unjust, fit into the political history of banditry, which makes bandits men of power, who are logically drawn into the universe of power? That is what I hope to show in the following chapters.

2
***

What is Social Banditry?

We are sad, it is true, but that is because we have always been persecuted. The gentry use the pen, we the gun; they are the lords of the land, we of the mountain.

An old brigand from Roccamandolfi[1]

If a typical brigand wants a long career he must be or show himself to be a philanthropist, even as he kills and robs to the best of his ability. Otherwise he risks losing popular sympathy and being taken for a common murderer or robber.[2]

For the law, anyone belonging to a group of men who attack and rob with violence is a bandit, from those who snatch payrolls at an urban street corner to organized insurgents or guerrillas who happen not to be officially recognized as such. They are today apt to be described, equally uncritically, as 'terrorists', a sign of the historic decline of the bandit image in the second half of the twentieth century. Historians and sociologists cannot use so crude a definition. In this book we shall be dealing only with some kinds of robbers, namely those who are *not* or not only regarded as simple criminals by public opinion. We shall be dealing essentially with a form of individual or minority rebellion within peasant societies. For the sake of convenience we shall omit the urban equivalent of the peasant bandit-rebel, and say little about the more numerous rural desperadoes who are not peasants by origin or allegiance, but impoverished gentlemen-robbers. Town and country are too different as human communities to be easily discussed in the same terms, and in any case peasant bandits, like most peasants, distrust and hate townsmen. Bandit gentry (most familiar in the form of the 'robber knights' of late medieval Germany) are much more mixed up with peasants, but the relationship, which will be discussed below (pp. 41–2, 98–101) is obscure and complex.

The point about social bandits is that they are peasant outlaws whom the lord and state regard as criminals, but who remain within peasant society, and are considered by their people as heroes, as champions, avengers, fighters for justice, perhaps even leaders of liberation, and in any case as men to be admired, helped and supported. In the cases where a traditional society resists the encroachments and historical advance of central governments and states, native or foreign, they may be helped and supported even by the local lords. This relation between the ordinary peasant and the rebel, outlaw and robber is what makes social banditry interesting and significant. It also distinguishes it from two other kinds of rural crime: from the activities of gangs drawn from the professional 'underworld' or of mere freebooters ('common robbers'), and from communities for whom raiding is part of the normal way of life, such as for instance the Bedouin. In both these cases victims and attackers are strangers and enemies. Underworld robbers and raiders regard the peasants as their prey and know them to be hostile; the robbed in turn regard the attackers as criminals in their sense of the term and not merely by official law. It would be unthinkable for a social bandit to snatch the peasants' (though not the lord's) harvest in his own territory, or perhaps even elsewhere. Those who do, therefore lack the peculiar relationship which makes banditry 'social'. Of course in practice such distinctions are often less clear than in theory. A man may be a social bandit on his native mountains, a mere robber on the plains. Nevertheless, analysis requires us to establish the difference.

Social banditry of this kind is one of the most universal social phenomena known to history, and one of the most amazingly uniform. Practically all cases belong to two or three clearly related types, and the variations within these are relatively superficial. What is more, this uniformity is not the consequence of cultural diffusion, but the reflection of similar situations within peasant societies, whether in China, Peru, Sicily, the Ukraine, or Indonesia. Geographically it is found throughout the Americas, Europe, the Islamic world, South and East Asia, and even Australia. Socially it seems to occur in all types of human society which lie between the evolutionary phase of tribal and kinship organization, and modern capitalist and industrial society, but including the phases of disintegrating kinship society and transition to agrarian capitalism.

Tribal or kinship societies are familiar with raiding, but lack the internal stratification which creates the bandit as a figure of social protest and rebellion. However, when such communities, especially those familiar with feuding and raiding such as hunters and pastoralists, develop their own systems of class differentiation, or when they are absorbed into larger economies resting on class conflict, they may supply a disproportionately large number of social bandits, as in the fifteenth- to eighteenth-century Ottoman Empire, where some historians have virtually identified brigandage and herdsmen. The best nineteenth-century examples are the Barbagia zone of Sardinia and the Hungarian Kuncsàg (the region of the Cumans, one of the last groups of Central Asian pastoral nomads to settle in Europe). In studying such regions it is hard to say at precisely what point the practice of raiding and feuding passes into social banditry, whether in the form of resistance to the rich, to foreign conquerors or oppressors, or to other forces destroying the traditional order of things – all of which may be linked in the minds of bandits, and indeed in reality. However, with luck we may be able to fix the transition chronologically to within one or two generations, e.g. in the Sardinian highlands to the half-century from the 1880s to the 1930s.

At the other end of historic development, modern agrarian systems, both capitalist and post-capitalist, are no longer those of traditional peasant society and cease to produce social bandits except in countries of what has been called 'settler capitalism' – the USA, Australia, Argentina. The country which has given the world Robin Hood, the international paradigm of social banditry, has no record of actual social bandits after, say, the early seventeenth century, though public opinion continued to find a more or less unsuitable substitute in the idealization of other kinds of criminal, such as highwaymen. In a broader sense 'modern-ization', that is to say the combination of economic development, efficient communications and public adminis-tration, deprives any kind of banditry, including the social, of the conditions under which it flourishes. In Tsarist Russia, for instance, where brigandage was endemic or epidemic over most of the country until the middle of the eighteenth century, by the end of that century it had disappeared from the immediate neighbourhood of towns, and by the middle of the nineteenth it had, speaking generally, retreated to unsettled and unpacified regions, especially those inhabited by minority peoples. The abolition of serfdom in 1861 marked the end of the long series of government decrees against banditry; the last seems to have been promulgated in 1864.

Otherwise social banditry is universally found wherever societies are based on agriculture (including pastoral econo-mies), and consist largely of peasants and landless labourers ruled, oppressed and exploited by someone else – lords, towns, governments, lawyers, or even banks. It is found in one or other of its three main forms, each of which will be discussed in a separate chapter: the *noble robber* or Robin Hood, the primitive resistance fighter or guerrilla unit of what I shall call the *haiduks*, and possibly the terror-bringing *avenger.*[*]

How common such banditry is, cannot be easily discovered. Though the sources give us plenty of examples of bandits, we rarely find estimates for the total numbers active at any one time or quantitative comparisons between the amounts of banditry at different times. We must, of course, distinguish between the normal grassroots outlawry and the regions and historical periods when, for one reason or another, large and lasting armed bands can maintain themselves, or those communities which organize their lives by a regular combination of agrarian pursuits and banditry. For instance the (Roman Catholic) Albanian Mirditi, were sadly described by their visiting bishop in 1703 as 'di genio bellicosa, dediti alle rapine, alli assassini' ('Of a warlike disposition and given to robbery and homicide') or the 'bandit villages' in the western Henan mountains in China. In periods of government breakdown, as in the post-imperial war-lord era of China, the numbers could be large. Taking a Japanese estimate for the middle 1920s as a base, one might guess that they amounted to between 0.5 per cent and 0.8 per cent of the total population in Manchuria, between 0.7 per cent and 1 per cent in Henan and Shandong, not counting the 1.5 million soldiers (in all China), largely recruited from, or potential, bandits. But this is quite exceptional. In 1962,

---

[*] A possible or partial exception might have to be made for the peculiar caste-divided societies of Hindu southern Asia, where social banditry is inhibited by the tendency of robbers, like all other sections of society, to form self-contained castes and communities. However, as we shall see, there are affinities between some kinds of dacoits and social bandits.

after the end of the most murderous phase of political conflict in Colombia, the six most disturbed departments of that country contained 161 bands with 2,760 members (police estimates). While this is a larger number than given in earlier editions of the book, it can hardly amount to more than one in a thousand of the total population of the regions affected.[3] Macedonia in the early twentieth century supported a distinctly larger number of bands among its population of, say, one million, but since these were largely financed and organized by various governments, they also represent far more than the spontaneous banditry to be expected in such an area. Even so, it is doubtful whether there were ever more than one or two thousand.[4]

Quite clearly the normal amount of banditry was modest. In nineteenth-century Corsica the maximum number of 'fugitives' counted or bandits estimated (for 355 villages) was 600. 200–300 is a more likely figure. (As late as 1933 there were still supposed to be one hundred outlaws on the island.)[5] In 1847, a moderately disturbed year, there were, according to the authorities, 600–700 active brigands in 50–60 small bands in Calabria, traditionally a region given to banditry.[6] Its total, and overwhelmingly rural population at the time was probably about one million. If we guess that bandits form no more than 0.1 per cent of the rural population at the outside, we are almost certainly making an ultra-generous estimate.

There are, of course, notable regional variations. They are partly due to geography, partly to technology and administration, partly to social and economic structure. It is a commonplace that brigands flourish in remote and inaccessible areas such as mountains, trackless plains, fenland, forest or estuaries with their labyrinth of creeks and waterways, and are attracted by trade-routes and major highways, where pre-industrial travel is naturally both slow and cumbrous. The construction of good and fast modern roads is often enough to diminish banditry notably. Administrative inefficiency and complication favour it. It is no accident that the Habsburg Empire in the nineteenth century managed its bandit problem more successfully than the ramshackle and effectively decentralized Turkish Empire, or that frontier regions – better still, regions of multiple frontiers like central Germany or the parts of India divided between the British and numerous princely states – were in perpetual difficulties. The ideal situation for robbery is one in which the local authorities are local men, operating in complex local situations, and where a few miles may put the robber beyond the reach or even the knowledge of one set of authorities and into the territory of another, which does not worry about what happens 'abroad'. Lists of areas peculiarly associated with banditry have been drawn up by historians, e.g. for Russia.[7]

Nevertheless, such obvious factors do not account entirely for the marked regional disparities in banditry which are usually found, and which led the Imperial Chinese criminal law, for instance, to establish the distinction between 'brigand areas' (such as the provinces of Sichuan, Henan, Anhui, Hubei, Shaanxi, parts of Kiangsu and Shandong) and others.[8] In the Peruvian departments of Tacna and Moquegua, which were otherwise very suitable, there was no banditry. Why? Because, argues a historian of the subject, 'here there are no landlords, truck-masters or labour contractors, no foremen, no full, absolute or irrevocable lordship over the water supplies'.[9] In other words, because peasant discontent was less. Conversely, an area like Bantam in north Java was a permanent centre of banditry in the nineteenth century, but it was also a permanent centre of rebellion. Only careful regional study can show why banditry was endemic in some parts, weak in other parts of the same country or region. Likewise, only detailed historical study can account for all its 'diachronic' variations. Still, the following generalizations can be made quite safely:

Banditry tended to become epidemic in times of pauperization and economic crisis. The striking increase in Mediterranean brigandage during the late sixteenth century, to which Fernand Braudel has drawn attention, reflected the striking decline in the peasants' condition of life at this period. The Aheriya of Uttar Pradesh (India), always a tribe of hunters, fowlers and thieves, 'did not take to highway robbery till the great famine of 1833'.[10] On a much shorter time-scale, banditry in the Sardinian highlands in the 1960s reached its peak each year when the shepherds' rent fell due. These observations are so platitudinous that they need merely be set down on paper to explain themselves. From the historian's point of view it is more illuminating to distinguish between those crises which signify major historical changes and those which do not, though the distinction will only be grasped slowly and retrospectively by the peasants concerned, if it ever becomes clear to them.

All rural societies of the past were accustomed to periodic dearth – harvest-failure and other natural crises – and to occasional catastrophes, unpredictable in themselves by the villagers, but likely to occur sooner or later, such as wars, conquests, or the breakdown of the administrative system of which they formed a small and remote part. All such catastrophes were likely to multiply banditry of one kind or another. All were likely to pass away, though political breakdowns and wars were also likely to leave behind bands of marauders or other desperadoes for a considerable period, especially if governments were weak or divided. An efficient modern state like France after the Revolution could liquidate the huge epidemic of (non-social) brigandage which swept the Rhineland during the 1790s, in a few years. On the other hand the social disruption of the Thirty Years War left behind in Germany a network of robber bands some of which persisted for at least another century. Nevertheless, so far as rural society is concerned, things tend to return to normal (including the normally expected amount of social and other banditry) after such traditional disturbances of equilibrium.

The situation is rather different when the events which precipitate an epidemic of banditry are not – to use geographical similes – comparable to earthquakes in Japan or floods in the Low Countries, but reflect long-term changes like the advance of glaciers in an ice-age, or irreversible ones like soil erosion. In such circumstances epidemics of banditry represent more than the simple multiplication of able-bodied men who take what they need by arms rather than starve. They may reflect the disruption of an entire society, the rise of new classes and social structures, the resistance of entire communities or peoples against the destruction of its way of life. Or they may reflect, as in the history of China, the exhaustion of the 'mandate of heaven', the social breakdown which is not due to adventitious forces, but marks the approaching end of a relatively long cycle of history, heralding the fall of one dynasty and the rise of another. Banditry at such times may be the precursor or companion of major social movements such as peasant revolutions. Alternatively, it may itself change by adapting to the new social and political situation, though in doing so it will almost certainly cease to be social banditry. In the typical case of the past two centuries, the transition from a pre-capitalist to a capitalist economy, the social transformation may entirely destroy the kind of agrarian society which gives birth to bandits, the kind of peasantry which nourishes them, and in doing so conclude the history of what is the subject of this book. The nineteenth and twentieth centuries have been the great age of social banditry in many parts of the world, just as the sixteenth to eighteenth probably were in most parts of Europe. Yet it is now largely extinct, except in a few areas.

In Europe it persists on any scale only in the Sardinian highlands, though the aftermath of two bouts of world war and revolution revived it in several regions. Yet in southern Italy, the classic country of the *banditi*, it reached its peak only a century ago, in the great peasant rebellion and guerrilla war of the brigands (1861–5). In Spain, the other classic country of bandits, it was familiar to every nineteenth-century traveller. It still occurs as an expected hazard of tourism in the Edwardian era in Bernard Shaw's *Man and Superman*. However, it was already drawing to an end there. Francisco Ríos ('El Pernales') who operated at this time is the last really legendary brigand of Andalusia. In Greece and the Balkans it is an even more recent memory. In north-east Brazil, where it entered its epidemic phase after 1870, and reached its peak in the first third of the twentieth century, it ended in 1940 and has not revived since. There are certainly regions – perhaps mainly in South and East Asia and one or two parts of Latin America – where old-style social banditry may still be found here and there, and it may arise in sub-Saharan Africa on a more significant scale than we have had record of in the past. But on the whole social banditry is a phenomenon of the past, though often of the very recent past. The modern world has killed it, though it has substituted its own forms of primitive rebellion and crime.

What part, if any, do bandits play in these transformations of society? As individuals, they are not so much political or social rebels, let alone revolutionaries, as peasants who refuse to submit, and in doing so stand out from their fellows, or even more simply, men who find themselves excluded from the usual career of their kind, and therefore forced into outlawry and 'crime'. *En masse*, they are little more than symptoms of crisis and tension in their society – of famine, pestilence, war or anything else that disrupts it. Banditry itself is therefore not a programme for peasant society but a form of self-help to escape it in particular circumstances. Bandits, except for their willingness or capacity to refuse individual submission, have no ideas other than those of the peasantry (or the section of the peasantry) of which they form a part. They are activists and not ideologists or prophets from whom novel visions or plans of social and political organization are to be expected. They are leaders, in so far as tough and self-reliant men often with strong personalities and military talents are likely to play such a role; but even then their function is to hack out the way and not to discover it. Several of the brigand chiefs of southern Italy in the 1860s, such as Crocco and Ninco Nanco,* showed gifts of generalship which won the admiration of the officers who fought them, but though the 'years of the brigands' are one of the rare examples of a major peasant rising captained by social banditry, at no stage did the brigand leaders appear to ask their followers to occupy the land, and sometimes they even appeared incapable of conceiving of what would today be called 'agrarian reform'.

Insofar as bandits have a 'programme', it is the defence or restoration of the traditional order of things 'as it should be' (which in traditional societies means as it is believed to have

---

* 'Crocco' (Carmine Donatelli), a farm-labourer and cowherd, had joined the Bourbon army, killed a comrade in a brawl, deserted and lived as an outlaw for ten years. He joined the liberal insurgents in 1860 in the hope of an amnesty for his past offences, and subsequently became the most formidable guerrilla chief and leader of men on the Bourbon side. He later escaped to the Papal States, was handed over to the Italian government and sentenced to life-imprisonment. In jail, many years later, he wrote an interesting autobiography. 'Ninco Nanco' (Giuseppe Nicola Summa), a landless labourer from Avigliano, had escaped from jail during the Garibaldian liberation of 1860. As Crocco's lieutenant he also demonstrated brilliant gifts as a guerrilla. Killed in 1864.

been in some real or mythical past). They right wrongs, they correct and avenge cases of injustice, and in doing so apply a more general criterion of just and fair relations between men in general, and especially between the rich and the poor, the strong and the weak. This is a modest aim, which leaves the rich to exploit the poor (but no more than is traditionally accepted as 'fair'), the strong to oppress the weak (but within the limits of what is equitable, and mindful of their social and moral duties). It demands not that there should be no more lords, or even that lords should not be expected to take their serfs' women, but only that when they did, they should not shirk the obligation to give their bastards an education.* In this sense social bandits are reformers, not revolutionaries.

However, reformist or revolutionary, banditry itself does not constitute a social *movement*. It may be a surrogate for it, as when peasants admire Robin Hoods as their champions, for want of any more positive activity by themselves. It may even be a substitute for it, as when banditry becomes institutionalized among some tough and combative section of the peasantry and actually inhibits the development of other means of struggle. Whether such cases occur has not been clearly established, but there is some evidence that they may. Thus in Peru, the pressure of the peasantry for land reform was (and in 1971 still remained) notably weaker in the departments of Huanuco and Apurimac, where agrarian problems were by no means less acute, but where there was (and is) a very deeply rooted tradition of cattle-rustling and brigandage. However, the question awaits serious investigation, like so many other aspects of banditry.†

Two things may, however, turn this modest, if violent, social objective of bandits – and the peasantry to whom they

---

* I take this example from actual conversations with peasants in Peru.

† I am grateful to Dr Mario Vasquez, Enrique Mayer, and various officials of Zone X of Agrarian Reform (central Peru) for some relevant information.

belong – into genuine revolutionary movements. The first is, when it becomes the symbol, even the spearhead, of resistance by the whole of the traditional order against the forces which disrupt and destroy it. A social revolution is no less revolutionary because it takes place in the name of what the outside world considers 'reaction' against what it considers 'progress'. The bandits of the kingdom of Naples, like its peasantry, who rose against the Jacobins and the foreigners in the name of Pope, King and the Holy Faith were revolutionaries, as Pope and King were not. (As an unusually sophisticated brigand leader in the 1860s told a captive lawyer, who claimed that he too was for the Bourbons: 'You're an educated man and a lawyer: do you really believe we're breaking our bones for Francis II?'*)[11] They rose not for the *reality* of the Bourbon kingdom – many of them had indeed helped to overthrow it a few months previously under Garibaldi – but for the ideal of the 'good old' society naturally symbolized by the ideal of the 'good old' church and 'good old' king. Bandits in politics tend to be such revolutionary traditionalists.

The second reason why bandits become revolutionaries is inherent in peasant society. Even those who accept exploitation, oppression and subjection as the norm of human life dream of a world without them: a world of equality, brotherhood and freedom, a totally *new* world without evil. Rarely is this more than a dream. Rarely is it more than an apocalyptic expectation, though in many societies the millennial dream persists: the Just Emperor will one day appear, the Queen of the South Seas will one day land (as in the Javanese version of this submerged hope), and all will be changed and perfect. Yet there are moments when the

---

*Admittedly Cipriano La Gala, an illiterate 'dealer' from Nola, sentenced for robbery with violence in 1855, escaped from jail in 1860, was not typical of the peasant brigands.

apocalypse seems imminent; when the entire structure of the state and existing society whose total end the apocalypse symbolizes and predicts, actually looks about to collapse in ruins, and the tiny light of hope turns into the light of a possible sunrise.

At such moments bandits are also swept away, like everyone else. Are they not blood of the people's blood? Are they not men who, in their own limited way, have shown that the wild life in the greenwood can bring liberty, equality and fraternity to those who pay the price of homelessness, danger and almost certain death? (The Brazilian *cangaçeiro* [bandit] bands have been seriously compared by a modern sociologist to 'a sort of brotherhood or lay confraternity', and observers were struck by the unparalleled honesty of personal relations within the bands.)[12] Do they not, consciously or unconsciously, recognize the superiority of the millennial or revolutionary movement to their own activities?

Indeed, nothing is more striking than this subordinate coexistence of banditry with major peasant revolution, of which it thus often serves as a precursor. The area of Andalusia traditionally associated with *bandoleros*, 'noble' or otherwise, became the area traditionally associated with rural anarchism a decade or two after their decline. The *sertão*** of north-eastern Brazil, which was the classical home of the *cangaçeiros*, was also that of the *santos*, the rural messianic leaders. Both flourished together, but the saints were greater. The great bandit Lampião, in one of the innumerable ballads which celebrate his exploits,

> Swore to be avenged on all
> Saying in this world I'll respect
> Father Cicero and no one else.[13]

* The back country of north-eastern Brazil beyond the frontiers of concentrated settlement.

And it was, as we shall see, from Father Cicero, the Messiah of Juazeiro, that public opinion derived Lampião's 'official' credentials. Social banditry and millenarianism – the most primitive forms of reform and revolution – go together historically. And when the great apocalyptic moments come, the brigand bands, their numbers swollen by the time of tribulation and expectation, may insensibly turn into something else. They may, as in Java, merge with the vast mobilizations of villagers who abandon field and house to rove the countryside in exalted hope; they may, as in southern Italy in 1861, find themselves expanding into peasant armies. They may, like Crocco in 1860, cease to be bandits and become soldiers of the revolution.

When banditry thus merges into a large movement, it becomes part of a force which can and does change society. Since the horizons of social bandits are narrow and circumscribed, like those of the peasantry itself, the results of their interventions into history may not be those they expected. They may be the opposite of what they expected. But this does not make banditry any less of a historical force. And in any case, how many of those who made the great social revolutions of the world foresaw the actual results of their endeavours?

3

***

Who Becomes a Bandit?

In Bulgaria only shepherds, cowmen and haiduks are free.

Panayot Hitov[1]

Banditry is freedom, but in a peasant society few can be free. Most are shackled by the double chains of lordship and labour, the one reinforcing the other. For what makes peasants the victims of authority and coercion is not so much their economic vulnerability – they are indeed as often as not virtually self-sufficient – as their immobility. Their roots are in the land and the homestead, and there they must stay like trees, or rather like sea-anemones or other sessile aquatic animals which settle down after a phase of youthful mobility. Once a man is married and on his holding, he is tied. The fields must be sown and harvested: even peasant rebellions must stop for the getting in of crops. The fences cannot be left too long unmended. Wife and children anchor a man to an identifiable spot. Only catastrophe, the approach of the millennium, or the grave decision to emigrate, can interrupt the fixed cycle of farming life, but even the emigrant must soon settle down again on some other holding, unless he ceases to be a peasant. The peasant's back is bent socially, because it must generally be bent in physical labour on his field.

This seriously limits the recruitment of bandits. It does not make it impossible for an adult peasant to turn bandit, but nevertheless it is very difficult, all the more so as the annual cycle of robbery follows the same rhythm as that of agriculture, being at its height in spring and summer, in recess during the bare and snowy seasons. (However, communities for whom raiding provides a regular part of their income must combine it with agriculture or pastoralism, and hence their banditry occurs during the off-season, as with the tribal *chuars** of Midnapur [Bengal] in the early nineteenth century; or else it is carried out by special raiding parties, who leave behind enough people to carry out the agricultural work.) If we want to understand the social composition of banditry, we must therefore look primarily at the mobile margin of peasant society.

The first and probably the most important source of bandits is in those forms of rural economy or rural environment which have relatively small labour demands, or which are too poor to employ all their able-bodied men; in other words, in the rural surplus population. Pastoral economies and areas of mountain and poor soil, which often go together, provide a permanent surplus of this kind, which tends to develop its own institutionalized outlets in traditional societies: seasonal emigration (as from the Alps or the Kabyle mountains in Algeria), the supply of soldiers (as in Switzerland, Albania, Corsica and Nepal), raiding or banditry. 'Minifundism' (i.e. the prevalence of holdings too small to maintain a family) may have the same effect. So, for even more obvious reasons, may landlessness. The rural proletarian, unemployed for a large part of the year, is 'mobilizable' as the peasant is not. Of the 328 'brigands' (or rather, rural insurgents and guerrillas) whose cases were up for review in 1863 by the Court of Appeal in Catanzaro (Calabria, Italy),

---

*Agricultural-cum-raiding tribesmen of the jungle districts in Midnapur (Bengal).

201 were described as farm-hands or day-labourers, only fifty-one as peasants, four as farmers, twenty-four as artisans.[2] It is obvious that in such environments there are not only plenty of men who can cut loose, at least for a period, from the rural economy, but who *must* look for other sources of income. Nothing is more natural than that some of them should become bandits, or that mountain and pastoral regions in particular should be the classical zones for such outlawry.

Even so, not everyone in such regions is equally likely to become an outlaw. However, there are always groups whose social position gives them the necessary freedom of action. The most important of them is the age-group of male youth between puberty and marriage, i.e. before the weight of full family responsibilities has begun to bend men's backs. (I am told that in countries which permit easy unilateral divorce, the time between the casting-off of one wife and remarriage may be another such episode of relative freedom, but, as with the analogous situation of widowers, this can only be so where there are no small children to be looked after, or where kinsfolk can be got to take care of them.) Even in peasant societies, youth is a phase of independence and potential rebellion. Young men, often united in formal or informal age-bands, can move from job to job, fight and rove. The *szégeny légeny* ('poor lads') of the Hungarian plains were such potential brigands; harmless enough in isolation, though not disinclined to rustle a head of horse or two, but when united in bands of twenty to thirty with their head-quarters in some secluded spot, easily passing over into banditry. 'The vast majority' of Chinese bandit recruits were young men because 'the short period before they assumed the burdens of marriage and family was the time when they were freer than they had ever been or ever would be again.' Hence also thirty was the crucial age when bandits were urged to leave the trade and settle down, and non-bandits who had failed to marry and settle down had little option but living on the margins of society.[3] One might add that their number was swollen by the selective infanticide of girl babies which might, as in some Chinese regions, produce a 20 per cent surplus of males over females. At all events there is no doubt whatever that the typical bandit was a young man and his equivalent, e.g. the Colombian guerrillas of the 1990s, almost all between 15 and 30, still is.[4] Two-thirds of the bandits in the Basilicata of the 1860s were under twenty-five years old. Forty-nine out of fifty-nine bandits in Lambayeque (Peru) were bachelors.[5] Diego Corrientes, the classical ban-dit legend of Andalusia, died at twenty-four, Janošik, his Slovak equivalent, at twenty-five, Lampião, the great *cangaçeiro* of the Brazilian north-east, started his career between the ages of seventeen and twenty, the real-life Don José of Carmen at the age of eighteen. The average age of Manchurian bandit chiefs in the 1920s was 25–26 years. Writers can be good observers: 'Slim Mehmed', the hero of a Turkish bandit-novel, went into the Taurus Mountains as a teenager.

The second most important source of free men are those who, for one reason or another, are not integrated into rural society and are therefore also forced into marginality or outlawry. The bands of *rasboiniki* (bandits) who flourished in the trackless and thinly-populated spaces of old Russia were composed of such marginal men – often migrants making for the open spaces of the south and east, where lordship, serfdom and government had not yet arrived, in search of what was later to become the consciously revolutionary prospect of *Zemlya i Volya* (Land and Freedom). Some of them did not get there at all, and they all had to live while moving along. So the escaped serfs, ruined freemen, run-aways from state or seignorial factories, from jail, seminary, army or navy, men with no determined place in society such as priests' sons, formed or joined brigand bands, which might merge with the raiding of former frontier communities of free peasants such as the Cossacks and national or tribal minorities. (For Cossacks, see Chapter 8 below.)

Among such marginals, soldiers, deserters and ex-service-men played a significant part. There was good reason for the Tsar to conscript his soldiers for life, or what amounted to life, so that their kinsfolk read the funeral service over them as they bade them farewell at the end of the village. Men who come back from afar, masterless and landless, are a danger to the stability of the social hierarchy. Ex-servicemen like deserters are natural material for banditry. Time and again the leaders of the brigands in southern Italy after 1860 are described as 'ex-soldier of the Bourbon army' or 'landless labourer, ex-soldier'. Indeed, in some areas this transforma-tion was normal. Why, asked a progressive Bolivian in 1929, do the ex-servicemen who return to their settlements among the Aymara Indians not act as educators and agents of civilization instead of 'turning into loafers and degenerates who become leaders of the bandits of this region'?[6] The question was just, but rhetorical. Ex-servicemen *can* act as leaders, educators and village cadres, and all socially revolu-tionary regimes use their armies as training schools for this purpose, but who would have really expected this in feudal Bolivia?

Few except returned ex-soldiers are entirely if temporarily outside the village economy, though still part of peasant society (as gypsies, and other *fahrendes Volk* or vagrants normally are not). However, the rural economy provides for a number of jobs which are outside the common routine of labour and the immediate range of social control, whether by the rulers or the public opinion of the ruled. There are, once again, the herdsmen, alone or with others of their kind – a special, sometimes a secret group – on the high pastures during the season of summer pasture, or roving as semi-nomads across the wide plains. There are the armed men and field-guards, whose job is not to labour, the drovers, carters and smugglers, bards and others of the kind. They are not watched, but rather watchers themselves. Indeed, as often as not the mountains provide their common world, into which landlords and ploughmen do not enter, and where men do not talk much about what they see and do. Here bandits meet shepherds, and shepherds consider whether to become bandits.

The sources of potential bandits we have considered so far are all collectives, that is to say social categories of men any one of whom is more likely to become a bandit than any one of the members of some other category. They are clearly very important. For instance, they enable us to make brief, approximate, but not fundamentally misleading generalizations such as: 'The characteristic bandit unit in a highland area is likely to consist of young herdsmen, landless labourers and ex-soldiers and unlikely to contain married men with children or artisans.' Such formulae do not exhaust the question, but they do cover a surprisingly large part of the field. For instance, of the south Italian band-leaders in the 1860s, those for whom we have occupational descriptions include twenty-eight 'shepherds', 'cowherds', 'ex-servicemen', 'landless labourers' and 'field guards' (or combinations of these occupations) and only five others.[7] However, it must be noted that bandit leaders, as distinct from the other ranks, are more likely to come from among these 'others', that is to say from strata of rural society above the proletarian and property-less. Nevertheless, there is another category of potential bandits, in some ways the most important, membership of which is, as it were, individual and voluntary, though it may well overlap with the others. This consists of the men who are unwilling to accept the meek and passive social role of the subject peasant; the stiff-necked and recalcitrant, the individual rebels. They are, in the classic familiar peasant phrase, the 'men who make themselves respected'.

There may not be many of them in ordinary peasant society, but there are always some. These are the men who, when faced with some act of injustice or persecution, do not yield meekly to force or social superiority, but take the path of resistance and outlawry. For we must remember that, if resistance to such acts of oppression is the characteristic start of a 'noble' robber's career, for every resister there must be scores who accept injustice. A Pancho Villa who claims to defend the honour of a raped sister is the exception in societies in which lords and their henchmen do as they will with peasant girls. These are the men who establish their right to be respected against all comers, including other peasants, by standing up and fighting – and in so doing automatically usurp the social role of their 'betters' who, as in the classic medieval ranking system, have the monopoly of fighting. They may be the toughs, who advertise their toughness by their swagger, their carrying of arms, sticks or clubs, even when peasants are not supposed to go armed, by the casual and rakish costume and manner which symbolize toughness. The 'bare-stick' of the old Chinese village (commonly translated as 'village bully' by old China hands) wore his pigtail loose, its end coiled round head and neck; his shoes deliberately down-at-heel; his leggings open to allow the expensive lining to show. He was often said to provoke the magistrate 'out of sheer bravado'.[8] The *vaquero* (or cowpuncher) outfit of the Mexican herd-riders which has become the classic cowboy costume of the Westerns, and the more or less equivalent styles of *gauchos* and *llaneros* on the South-American plains, *bétyars** on the Hungarian *puszta*,

* *Gauchos, llaneros*: Argentinian and Colombian cowboys. *Bétyars*: masterless and outcast men.

majos and *flamencos** in Spain, are examples of similar symbols of unsubmissiveness in the Western world. Such symbolism reached perhaps its most elaborate expression in the gold- and steel-festooned costume of the Balkan haiduk or *klepht*. For, as in all traditional and slow-changing societies, even the loose group of the non-conformist poor becomes formalized and recognized by outward signs. The rural tough's outfit is a code which reads: 'This man is not tame.'

Those 'who make themselves respected' do not automatic-ally become bandits, or at least not social bandits. They may fight their way out of the peasant's lot by becoming village guards, lord's retainers or soldiers (which means official bandits of various kinds). They may look after themselves and become a strong-arm rural bourgeoisie, like the *Mafiosi* of Sicily. They may also become the kind of outlaws about whom men sing ballads: champions, heroes and avengers. Theirs is an individual rebellion, which is socially and politic-ally undetermined, and which under normal – i.e. non-revolutionary – conditions is not a vanguard of mass revolt, but rather the product and counterpart of the general passivity of the poor. They are the exception which proves the rule.

These categories more or less exhaust the sources which supply peasant bandits. However, we must briefly consider two other reservoirs of rural violence and robbery, which are sometimes rightly, but in most cases quite mistakenly, confused with peasant banditry: 'robber barons' and crim-inals.

It stands to reason that impoverished country gentlemen provide an endless supply of toughs. Arms are their privilege, fighting their vocation and the basis of their system of values. A good deal of this violence is institutionalized in such

---

* *Majo* and *flamenco* are descriptions of a style of dress and behaviour summarized in an eighteenth-century Spanish dictionary as 'the man who affects valour and panache in word and action'.

pursuits as hunting, the defence of personal and family 'honour' by duels and vengeance and suchlike, or channelled by careful governments into politically useful or at least harmless outlets such as military service and colonial adventure. Dumas's Musketeers, the products of that well-known nursery of impecunious gentlemen, Gascony, were plainly little more than officially licensed bullies with a pedigree, analogous to the peasant or shepherd roughnecks hired as guards by Italian or Iberian latifundists. So were many of the Spanish *conquistadores*. There are, however, situations in which such pauper squires become actual outlaws and robbers (see Chapter 7 below). We may guess that the outlaw gentleman is most likely to enter the realm of popular myth and ballad (a) when he can form part of a general movement of resistance by some archaic society against outsiders or foreign conquest; or (b) when there is only a feeble tradition of active peasant rebellion against seignorial injustice. He is least likely to enter it where the element of class struggle is most pronounced, though of course in countries with a high proportion of 'gentlemen', such as Poland, Hungary and Spain, where they formed perhaps ten per cent of the total population, they provided a large public for ballads and romances about themselves.[*]

There is an even sharper division between peasant bandits and the criminal underworld of urban or vagrant elements, which existed in the interstices of rural society but clearly did not belong to it. In traditional societies criminals are almost

[*] The classification of bandit songs and ballads is complicated by two factors. First, the tendency of 'official' culture to upgrade them socially as the price of assimilating them, i.e. to turn Robin Hood into a wronged Earl of Huntingdon; second, the tendency of all free men in feudal types of rural society to assimilate their own status to the only familiar model of 'freedom', i.e. the status of 'nobility'. Possibly the latter accounts for the belief that unquestioned Hungarian peasant bandits of the nineteenth century, like Sandor Rósza and Sóbry Jószi, were noblemen of old family; possibly the former.

by definition outsiders, who form their own separate society, if not actually an anti-society of the 'bent' which mirrors that of the 'straight'. They normally speak their own special language (argot, cant, *caló*, *Rotwelsch*). Their associations are with other outcast occupations or communities, like the gypsies, who supplied so much of the argot of the French and Spanish underworld, the Jews who provided even more vocabulary to the German. (The bulk of peasant bandits speak no kind of argot, but simply a version of the local peasant dialect.) They are non-conformists, or rather anti-conformists in practice and by ideology; on the devil's side rather than God's,[*][9] or if religious, then on the side of heresy against orthodoxy. In the seventeenth century Christian villains in Germany petitioned to join the religious services of the Jews in jail, and there is quite strong evidence (echoed in Schiller's play *The Robbers*) that eighteenth-century German bands provided a refuge for libertinist or antinomian sectarians, such as survivors of central-German anabaptism.[10] Peasant bandits are in no sense heterodox, but share the value-system of ordinary peasants, including their piety, and their suspicion of out groups. (Thus, except in the Balkans, most central and east European social bandits were anti-Semitic.)

Where bands of criminal robbers roam the countryside, as in parts of central Europe in the seventeenth and eighteenth centuries, or in India, they can therefore normally be distinguished from social bandits both by their composition and their mode of operation. They are likely to consist of members of 'criminal tribes and castes', or individuals from outcast groups. Thus the Crefeld and Neuss gang of the 1790s, like Keil's gang, was composed largely of knife-grinders, while in Hesse-Waldeck there was a gang com-

---

[*] 'A robber who had not made a pact with the devil was unthinkable, especially in the sixteenth century, and until recent times the devil has occupied the first place in the dogmatic system of the robbers.'

posed mainly of rag-and-bone men. About half of the Salembier gang which made the Pas-de-Calais unsafe in the same period were hawkers, dealers in second-hand goods, fairground people and the like. The formidable Low Countries gang, with most of its various sub-units, was largely Jewish. And so on. Criminal vocations were often hereditary: the Bavarian woman-robber Schattinger had a family tradition of two hundred years to look back upon, and more than twenty of her kin, including her father and sister, were in jail or had been executed.[11] It is not surprising that they did not seek the sympathy of the peasantry, since they, like all the 'straight' people, were their enemies, oppressors and victims. Criminal bands thus lacked the local roots of social bandits or at least concealed them, but at the same time they were not confined by the limits of the territory beyond which social bandits could rarely venture in safety. They formed part of large, if loose, networks of an underworld which might stretch over half a continent, and would certainly extend into the cities which were *terra incognita* for peasant bandits who feared and hated them. For vagrants, nomads, criminals and their like, the kind of area within which most social bandits lived out their lives was merely a location for so many markets or fairs a year, a place for occasional raids, or at most (for instance, if strategically placed near several frontiers) a suitable headquarters for wider operations.

Nevertheless, criminal robbers cannot be simply excluded from the study of social banditry. In the first place, where for one reason or another social banditry did not flourish or had died out, suitable criminal robbers might well be idealized and given the attributes of Robin Hood, especially when they concentrated on holding up merchants, rich travellers, and others who enjoyed no great sympathy among the poor. Thus in eighteenth-century France, England and Germany celebrated underworld characters like Dick Turpin, Cartouche and Schinderhannes substituted for the genuine Robin Hoods who had disappeared from these countries by that time.[*]

In the second place, involuntary outcasts from the peasantry, such as the ex-soldiers, deserters and marauders who abounded in periods of disorder, war or its aftermath, provided a link between social and anti-social banditry. Such men would have fitted easily into social bands, but attached themselves with equal ease to the others, bringing to them some of the values and assumptions of their native environment. In the third place, old-established and permanent pre-industrial empires had long developed a double underworld: not only that of the outcast, but also that of unofficial mutual defence and opposition, as typified by the great and long-lasting secret societies of Imperial China or Vietnam, or perhaps by bodies like the Sicilian Mafia. Such unofficial political systems and networks, which are still very poorly understood and known, might reach out to all who were outside and against the official structure of power, including both social bandits and the outsider groups. They might, for instance, provide both with the alliances and resources which, under certain circumstances, turned banditry into a nucleus of effective political rebellion.

However, though in practice social banditry cannot always be clearly separated from other kinds of banditry, this does not affect the fundamental analysis of the social bandit as a special type of peasant protest and rebellion. This is what forms the main subject of the present book.

[*]Dick Turpin, 1705–39; Cartouche, 1693–1721; 'Schinderhannes' (Johannes Pueckler), 1783–1803. The other French bandit hero of the eighteenth century, Robert Mandrin, 1724–55, was a somewhat less unsuitable candidate for idealization. He was a professional smuggler from the Franco-Swiss border region, a trade never considered criminal by anybody except governments; and he was engaged on a campaign of vengeance.

4

* * *

The Noble Robber

On that night the moon was dim and the light of the stars filled the sky. They had gone but a little more than three miles when they saw the crowd of carts and upon the banners over them was written clearly 'The grain of the righteous and Loyal Robbers' Lair'.

The Shui Hu Zhuan[1]

WICKED: A man who kills Christians without a deep reason.

From a word association test given to the famous Calabrian bandit Musolino[2]

Robin Hood, the noble robber, is the most famous and universally popular type of bandit, the most common hero of ballad and song in theory, though scarcely in practice.* There is no mystery in this disproportion between legend and fact, any more than there is in the divergence between the realities of medieval knighthood and the dream of chivalry. Robin Hood is what all peasant bandits should be, but in the nature of things, few of them have the idealism, the unselfishness, or the social consciousness to live up to their role, and perhaps even fewer can afford to. Still, the rare ones who live up to expectations or seem to – and genuine Robin Hoods have

---

* For the purposes of this book Robin Hood is pure myth. As it happens, though ballads about him go back to the fourteenth century, he was not commonly regarded as a hero until the sixteenth century. The question whether a real Robin Hood existed, or what medieval English bands were like in the greenwoods, must be left to experts in the history of the Middle Ages.

been known – enjoy the veneration due to heroes, even to saints. Diego Corrientes (1757–81), the noble robber of Andalusia, was, according to popular opinion, similar to Christ: he was betrayed, delivered to Seville on a Sunday, tried on a Friday in March, and yet had killed nobody.[3] The real Juro Janošik (1688–1713) was, like most social bandits, a provincial robber in some lost corner of the Carpathians whose existence would barely attract the attention of the authorities in the capital. But literally hundreds of songs about him survive to the present day. On the other hand, such is the need for heroes and champions, that if there are no real ones, unsuitable candidates are pressed into service. In real life most Robin Hoods were far from noble.

It is therefore as well to begin with the 'image' of the noble robber, which defines both his social role and his relationship with the common peasants. His role is that of the champion, the righter of wrongs, the bringer of justice and social equity. His relation with the peasants is that of total solidarity and identity. The 'image' reflects both. It may be summarized in nine points.

First, the noble robber begins his career of outlawry not by crime, but as the victim of injustice, or through being persecuted by the authorities for some act which they, but not the custom of his people, consider as criminal.

Second, he 'rights wrongs'.

Third, he 'takes from the rich to give to the poor'.

Fourth, he 'never kills but in self-defence or just revenge'.

Fifth, if he survives, he returns to his people as an honourable citizen and member of the community. Indeed, he never actually leaves the community.

Sixth, he is admired, helped and supported by his people.

Seventh, he dies invariably and only through treason, since no decent member of the community would help the authorities against him.

Eighth, he is – at least in theory – invisible and invulnerable.

Ninth, he is not the enemy of the king or emperor, who is the fount of justice, but only of the local gentry, clergy or other oppressors.

Indeed, the facts largely confirm the image, insofar as it represents reality and not wish-fulfilment. Social bandits do, in the great majority of recorded cases, begin their career with some non-criminal dispute, affair of honour or as victims of what they and their neighbours feel to be injustice (which may be no more than the automatic consequence of a dispute between one of the poor and one of the rich and influential). Angelo Duca or 'Angiolillo' (1760–84), a Neapolitan bandit of the eighteenth century, became an outlaw over some dispute about strayed cattle with a field-guard of the Duke of Martina; Pancho Villa in Mexico revenging the honour of his sister against a landowner; Labarêda, like practically all Brazilian *cangaçeiros*, over an affair of family honour; Giuliano as a young smuggler – as honourable a trade as any in the mountains – for resisting a revenue man whom he was too poor to bribe. And so on. And indeed it is essential for the Robin Hood to start in this way, for if he were to be a *real* criminal, by the moral standards of his community, how could he enjoy its unqualified support?

To begin as the victim of injustice is to be imbued with the need to right at least one wrong: the bandit's own. It is natural enough that real bandits often demonstrate that 'savage spirit of justice' which observers noted in José Maria 'El Tempranillo' (the original Don José of *Carmen*) who operated in the Andalusian hills. In the legend, this righting of wrongs often takes the form of a literal transfer of wealth. Jesse James (1847–82) is supposed to have lent a poor widow $800 to meet her debt to a banker, then to have held up the banker and taken the money back; an improbable story from all we know of the James brothers.[*] In extreme cases, as in Schiller's drama *The Robbers*, the noble bandit offers his own life in exchange for justice for some poor man. Just so in real life (or was it in contemporary legend?) Zelim Khan, the Robin Hood of early twentieth-century Daghestan, cornered in a mountain cave, sent word through a shepherd to the opposing commander:

> 'Go tell the chief of the district that I shall give myself up to him when he shows me a telegram on a paper from the Tsar saying he will withdraw all fines imposed on innocents; and furthermore that a free pardon will be issued to all detained and exiled on account of me. But if not, then tell Prince Karavlov that this very night, before midnight, I shall escape from this cave, in spite of everything and everyone. Till then I await his answer.'

In practice rough justice is more likely to take the form of vengeance and retribution. Zelim Khan, to quote him again, wrote to a Moslem officer, a certain Donugayev:

> Take note that I kill the representatives of authority because they have illegally exiled my poor people to Siberia. When Col. Popov was head of Grozniy district there was an uprising, and the representatives of authority and the army felt they had to assert themselves by massacring several poor unfortunates. When I heard this I assembled my band and looted a train at Kadi-Yurt. There I killed Russians for vengeance.'[4]

Whatever the actual practice, there is no doubt that the bandit is considered an agent of justice, indeed a restorer of morality, and often considers himself as such.

Whether he takes from the rich to give to the poor is a much-debated question, though it is evident that he cannot

[*] The identical story is told of Maté Cosido, the leading social bandit of the Argentine Chaco in the 1930s.

afford to take from the local poor if he is to retain their support against the authorities. There is no question that 'noble' bandits have the reputation of redistributing wealth. 'Banditry in Lambayeque has always been distinguished', writes Colonel of the *Guardia Civil* Victor Zapata, 'by its gallantry, valour, finesse and the disinterestedness of the brigands. Neither bloodthirsty nor cruel, these used, in most cases, to distribute their booty among the poor and hungry, thus showing that they were not lost to feelings of charity and had not hardened their hearts.'[5] The distinction between bandits who have this reputation and those who have not is very clear in the mind of the local population, including (as the above quotation suggests) the police itself. There is also no question that some bandits do sometimes give to the poor, whether in the form of individual beneficence or indiscriminate largesse. Pancho Villa distributed the proceeds of his first major coup as follows: 5,000 pesos to his mother, 4,000 to the families of relatives and

> I bought a tailor's shop for a man named Antonio Retana who had very poor eyesight and a large and needy family. I hired a man to run it and gave him the same amount of money. And so it went on. By the end of eight or ten months all that I had left of the 50,000 pesos went to help people in need.[6]

On the other hand Luis Pardo, the Robin Hood of Peruvian banditry (1874–1909) seems to have preferred scattering handfuls of silver among the crowds at fiestas, as in his native town of Chiquian, or 'sheets, soap, biscuits, tins of food, candles etc.', bought in the local shops, as in Llaclla.[7] No doubt, many bandits may have gained their reputation for generosity simply through paying generously for the services, food and shelter of the local population. This, at least, is the view of Esteban Montejo, an unromantic ancient Cuban disinclined to sentimentalize the bandits of his youth.[8] Still, even he admits that 'when they robbed a good big sum, they went and shared it out'. Naturally in pre-industrial societies liberality and charity are a moral obligation for the 'good' man of power and wealth. Sometimes, as among the dacoits of India, they are formally institutionalized. The Badhaks – most famous of robber communities in northern India – set aside 4,500 rupees out of a haul of 40,000 for sacrifice to the gods and charity. The Minas were celebrated for their charity.[9] Conversely, there are no ballads about the rather insolvent bandits of Piura, a fact which the student of Peruvian banditry explains by their being too poor to distribute their loot to the other poor. In other words, taking from the rich and giving to the poor is a familiar and established custom, or at least an ideal moral obligation, whether in the greenwood of Sherwood Forest or in the American south-west of Billy the Kid who, the story goes, 'was good to Mexicans. He was like Robin Hood; he'd steal from white people and give it to the Mexicans, so they thought he was all right.'[10]

Moderation in the use of violence is an equally important part of the Robin Hood image. 'He robs the rich, helps the poor and kills nobody', ran the phrase about Diego Corrientes of Andalusia. Ch'ao Kai, one of the bandit leaders in the classic Chinese Water-Margin novel, asks after a raid: 'Was no man killed?', and when told that nobody was hurt 'Ch'ao Kai, hearing this, was mightily pleased and said "From this day on we are not to injure people".'[11] Melnikov, an ex-Cossack operating near Orenburg 'killed but rarely'. The Catalan brigands of the sixteenth and seventeenth centuries, at least in the ballads, must kill only in defence of their honour; even Jesse James and Billy the Kid were required by their legend to kill only in self-defence or for other just causes. This abstention from wanton violence is all the more astonishing, since the sort of environment in which bandits operate is often one in which all men go armed, where killing is normal, and where in any case the safest maxim is to shoot first and ask questions later. In any case it is hard to suppose that any of their contemporaries who knew them seriously believed that the James brothers or Billy the Kid thought twice about killing anyone in their way.

Whether any real bandit was ever in a position to live consistently up to this moral requirement of his status is therefore very doubtful. Whether he was ever really expected to, is also by no means clear; for though the moral imperatives of a peasant society are sharp and defined, men used to poverty and helplessness usually make an equally sharp distinction between those commandments which are genuinely binding in virtually all circumstances – e.g. not talking to the police – and those which, from necessity or destitution, can be dispensed with.[*] And yet, the very familiarity of killing and violence makes men extremely sensitive to moral distinctions which escape more pacific societies. There is just or legitimate killing and unjust, unnecessary and wanton murder; there are honourable and shameful acts. This distinction applies both to the judgement of those who are the potential victims of armed violence, the peaceable submissive peasantry, and to the fighters themselves, whose code may well be a rough chivalry, which frowns on the killing of the helpless, and even on the 'unfair' attacks on recognized and open adversaries such as the *local* police, with whom the bandit may be linked in mutual respect. (The rules which apply to outsiders are rather different.)[†] Whatever the

[*] Juan Martinez Alier has made this point with great force on the basis of a series of interviews with rural labourers in Andalusia in 1964–5.[12]

[†] Yashar Kemal's novel *Mehmed My Hawk* gives some good illustrations of this relationship. The hero warns the local sergeant, who spends most of his time pursuing bandits, to take cover when he happens to surprise him. Conversely, the sergeant has cornered Mehmed in a mountain cave, with his wife, new-born baby and another woman. To save them Mehmed offers to give himself up. The sergeant advances to take his surrender, but one of the women taunts him: 'You think you have captured him in fair fight, but you have only won because he cannot let the

definition of 'just' killing, the 'noble bandit' must at least seek to remain within it, and it is probable that the true social bandit does. We shall have occasion later to consider the type of bandit to whom this limitation does not apply.

Since the social bandit is not a criminal, he has no difficulty in rejoining his community as a respected member when he ceases to be an outlaw.[‡] The documents are unanimous on this point. Indeed, he may never actually leave it. In most cases he is likely to operate within the territory of his village or kinsfolk, being maintained by them as a matter of family duty as well as common sense, for if they did not feed him, would he not be obliged to become a common robber? The point is made with equal conviction by a Habsburg student of Bosnia and a Corsican official of the French Republic: 'Better to feed them than that they should steal.'[14] In remote and inaccessible areas, where the agents of authority enter only on occasional forays, the bandit may actually live in the village, unless word should come that the police are on the way; thus in the wilds of Calabria or Sicily. Indeed in the real back country, where law and government leave only the faintest trace, the bandit may be not only tolerated and protected, but a leading member of the community, as often in the Balkans.

Consider the case of a certain Kota Christov of Roulia, in the depths of late-nineteenth-century Macedonia. He was the most feared band-leader of the region, but at the same time the recognized leading citizen of his village, its head-man, shopkeeper, innkeeper and jack of all trades. On behalf of his village he resisted the local (mostly Albanian) land-owners and defied the Turkish officials who came to

child die.' And the sergeant cannot bring himself to take the celebrated outlaw in, for there would be no glory in such a victory: he lets him escape.

[‡] Luis Borrego, companion to the famous 'El Tempranillo', even managed subsequently to become the mayor of the township of Benamejí; admittedly a settlement which has traditionally shown no bias against bandits.[13]

requisition food for soldiers and gendarmes, with whom he always passed the time of day and who never attempted to disturb him. A devout Christian, he knelt before the shrine at the Byzantine monastery of the Holy Trinity after every one of his exploits, and deplored the wanton killing of Christians, though not, we may suppose, Albanians of any religion.[*] Kota was unquestionably not a simple robber, and though extremely shaky by modern ideological standards – he fought first for the Turks, then for the Internal Macedonian Revolutionary Organization, later still for the Greeks – a systematic defender of 'his' people's rights against injustice and oppression. Moreover, he seems to have made a clear distinction between permissible and impermissible attacks, which may reflect either a sense of justice or of local politics; at all events he expelled two of his band for killing a certain Abdin Bey, though he had himself dispatched a number of other local tyrants. The only reason why such a man cannot be simply classified as a social bandit is that in the political conditions of Turkish Macedonia, he was hardly an outlaw at all, at least for most of the time. Where the bonds of government and lordship were loose, Robin Hood was a recognized community leader.

It is only natural that the people's champion should not only be, by local standards, honest and respectable, but entirely admirable. As we have seen, the Robin Hood 'image' insists on morally positive actions such as robbing the rich and not killing too much, but more than this, it insists on the standard attributes of the morally approved citizen. Peasant societies make very clear distinctions between the social bandits who deserve, or are believed to deserve, such approval, and those who, though sometimes celebrated, feared and even admired, do not. Several

[*] Curiously enough, he became a hero among the Albanians, who have a song about him.[15]

languages indeed have separate words for these different types of robbers. There are plenty of ballads which end with the famous robber confessing his sins on his deathbed, or atoning for his awful deeds, like the haiduk *voivode* Indje, whom the earth vomited forth three times before he found rest in his grave when a dead dog was placed in it with him.[16] That is not the fate of the noble robber, for he has committed no sin. On the contrary, the people pray for his safety, like the women of San Stefano in Aspromonte (Calabria) for the great Musolino.[17]

> Musolino is innocent.
> They have condemned him unjustly;
> Oh Madonna, oh Saint Joseph,
> Let him always be under your protection . . .
> Oh Jesus, oh my Madonna,
> Keep him from all harm
> Now and for ever, so let it be.

For the noble bandit is *good*. To take a case where reality and image are in some conflict, Jesse James was supposed never to have robbed preachers, widows, orphans or ex-Confederates. What is more, he was supposed to have been a devout Baptist who taught in a church singing school. The dirt-farmers of Missouri could hardly go further in establishing his moral bona fides.

Indeed, the good bandit can, after death, acquire the most ultimate moral standing, that of the intermediary between humans and divinity. A substantial number of the cults formed round the graves of *gaucho* toughs have been found in Argentina, mostly former fighters in the political civil wars of the nineteenth century turned brigands, their miracle-working graves often bearing the colours of their party.

A man of this sort would naturally be helped by one and all, and since nobody would help the law against him, and he would be virtually beyond discovery by clumsy soldiers and gendarmes in the country he knew so well, only treason could lead to his capture. As the Spanish ballad has it:

> Two thousand escudos of silver
> They will give for his head alone.
> Many would win the prize,
> But nobody can succeed,
> Only a comrade could.[18]

In practice as well as in theory bandits perish by treason, though the police may claim the credit, as with Giuliano. (There is even a Corsican proverb about this: 'Killed after death, like a bandit by the police'.) The ballads and tales are full of these execrated traitors, from the time of Robin Hood himself to the twentieth century: Robert Ford, who betrayed Jesse James, Pat Garrett, the Judas of Billy the Kid, or Jim Murphy who gave away Sam Bass:

> Oh what a scorching Jim will get
> When Gabriel blows his horn.

But so are the documented stories of the death of bandits: Oleksa Dovbuš, the Carpathian bandit of the eighteenth century, did not die through the betrayal of his mistress Eržika, as the songs have it, but was killed by the peasant Stepan Dzvinka, whom he had aided, shot in the back. Salvatore Giuliano was betrayed, and so were Angiolillo and Diego Corrientes. For how else could such men die?

Were they not invisible and invulnerable? 'People's bandits' are always believed to be, probably unlike other desperadoes, and the belief reflects their identification with the peasantry. They are always going about the countryside in impenetrable disguises, or in the dress of an ordinary man, unrecognized by the forces of authority until they reveal themselves. For since nobody will give them away and they are indistinguishable from common men, they are *as good as* invisible. The anecdotes merely give a symbolic expression to this relationship. Their invulnerability seems to be a somewhat more complex phenomenon. To some extent it also reflects the security which bandits have among their people and on their own ground. To some extent it expresses the wish that the people's champion cannot be defeated, the same sort of wish that produces the perennial myths of the good king – and the good bandit – who has not really died, but will come back one day to restore justice. Refusal to believe in a robber's death is a certain criterion of his 'nobility'. Thus Sergeant Romano was not really killed, but may still be seen roaming the countryside secretly and in solitude; Pernales (one of several Andalusian bandits about whom such stories are told) 'really' got away to Mexico; Jesse James to California. For the bandit's defeat and death is the defeat of his people; and what is worse, of hope. Men can live without justice, and generally must, but they cannot live without hope.

However, the bandit's invulnerability is not only symbolic. It is almost invariably due to magic, which reflects the beneficent interest of the divinities in his affairs. South Italian brigands had amulets blessed by Pope or King, and regarded themselves as being under the protection of the virgin; those of southern Peru appealed to Our Lady of Luren, those of north-eastern Brazil to the local holy men. In certain societies with strongly institutionalized brigandage, such as South and South-East Asia, the magical element is even more highly developed and its significance is perhaps clearer. Thus the traditional Javanese 'rampok' band is essentially a 'group formation of a magical–mystical nature', and its members are united, in addition to other bonds, by the *ilmoe* (elmu), a magical charm which may consist of a word, an amulet, an adage, but sometimes simply personal conviction, and which is in turn acquired by spiritual exercises, meditation and the like, by gift or purchase, or which comes to a man at birth, designating him for his vocation. It is this which makes robbers invisible and invulnerable, paralyses their victims or sends them to sleep, and allows them to fix, by divination, the place, day and hour of their exploits – but also forbids them to vary the plan once it has been divinely determined. The interesting point about this Indonesian bandit magic is that it can under certain circumstances be generalized. At moments of high millennial excitement, when the masses themselves rise in expectation, they also believe themselves to be magically invulnerable. Magic therefore may express the spiritual legitimacy of the bandit's action, the function of leadership in the band, the compelling force of the cause. But perhaps it may also be seen as a sort of double insurance policy: one which supplements human skill,* but which also explains human failure. For if the omens have been read wrongly, or one or other of the magical conditions have not been fulfilled, the defeat of the invulnerable hero does not imply the defeat of the ideal which he represents. And, alas, the poor and weak know that their champions and defenders are not really invulnerable. They may always rise again – but they will also be defeated and killed.

Finally, since the noble robber is just, he cannot be in real conflict with the fount of justice, whether divine or human. There are a number of versions of the story of conflict and reconciliation between bandit and king. The Robin Hood

---

* Indonesian bandit leaders have strong magic only if they also prove their fitness to lead by success in action; the Aheriya dacoits of Uttar Pradesh took omens before their robberies, but very brave *jemadars* (leaders) might not bother to.[19] A song about Lampião puts the matter very clearly, as usual. The great bandit was treated by Master Macumba, a *feiticeiro* (witch doctor or magician) with the African magic which, as all know, is the strongest, to make him invulnerable to gun and knife; but the wizard also told him, in case of need, to appeal to 'Saint Legs, St Vigilant, St Rifle, St Suspicious, St Lookout', etc.

cycle alone contains several. The king, on the advice of evil counsellors such as the Sheriff of Nottingham, pursues the noble outlaw. They fight, but the king cannot vanquish him. They meet and the ruler, who naturally recognizes the outlaw's virtue, allows him to continue his good work, or even takes him into his own service.[*] The symbolic meaning of these anecdotes is clear. It is less evident that, if not actually true, they may still rest on experiences which make them plausible enough to people in the kind of environments in which banditry abounds. Where the state is remote, ineffective and weak, it will indeed be tempted to come to terms with any local power-group it cannot defeat. If robbers are successful enough, they have to be conciliated just like any other centre of armed force. Every person who lives in times when banditry has got out of hand knows that local officials have to establish a working relationship with robber chiefs, just as every citizen of New York knows that the police has such relationships with the 'mobs' (see below p. 96). It is neither incredible nor unprecedented that famous bandits should be pardoned and given official posts by the king, e.g. El Tempranillo (Don José) in Andalusia. Nor is it incredible that Robin Hoods, whose ideology is precisely the same as that of the surrounding peasantry, should think of themselves as 'loyal and righteous'. The only difficulty is that the closer a bandit comes to the people's ideal of a 'noble robber', i.e. to being the socially conscious champion of the rights of the poor, the less likely is it that the authorities will open their arms to him. They are much more apt to treat him as a social revolutionary and hunt him down.

This should normally take them not more than two or three years, the average span of a Robin Hood's career, unless he operates in some very remote region and/or

---

[*] Historians have even tried to authenticate the existence of Robin Hood by searching the royal accounts for wages paid to an R. Hood by the king.

enjoys a very great deal of political protection.* For if the
authorities really bring in enough troops (the effect of
which is not so much to frighten the bandit but to make
the life of the peasants who support him miserable), and if
a sufficiently large reward is offered, then his days are
counted. Only modern, organized guerrilla war can resist
under such conditions; but Robin Hoods are very far from
modern guerrillas: partly because they operate as leaders of
small bands, helpless outside their native territory, partly
because they are organizationally and ideologically too
archaic.

Indeed, they are not even social or any kind of revolutionaries, though the true Robin Hood sympathizes with the
revolutionary aspirations of 'his' people and joins revolutions when be can. We shall consider this aspect of banditry
in a later chapter. However, his object is comparatively
modest. He protests not against the fact that peasants are
poor and oppressed. He seeks to establish or to re-establish
justice or 'the old ways', that is to say, fair dealing in a
society of oppression. He rights wrongs. He does not seek
to establish a society of freedom and equality. The stories
that are told about him record modest triumphs: a widow's
farm saved, a local tyrant killed, an imprisoned man set free,
an unjust death avenged. At most – and the case is rare
enough – he may, like Vardarelli in Apulia, order bailiffs to
give bread to their labourers, to permit the poor to glean, or
he may distribute salt free, i.e. to cancel taxes. (This is an
important function, which is why professional smugglers
like Mandrin, the hero of eighteenth-century French bandit
myth, may acquire the Robin Hood halo without difficulty.)

---

*Janošik lasted two years, Diego Corrientes three, Musolino two, most of the
south Italian brigands of the 1860s not more than two, but Giuliano (1922–50)
seven, until he lost the goodwill of the Mafia.

· The ordinary Robin Hood can do little more, though, as we shall see, there are societies in which banditry appears not simply in the form of the occasional hero who gathers about him the usual six to twenty men, but as a permanently established institution. In such countries the revolutionary potential of robbers is considerably greater (see Chapter 6). The traditional 'noble robber' represents an extremely primitive form of social protest, perhaps the most primitive there is. He is an individual who refuses to bend his back, that is all. Most men of his kind will, in non-revolutionary conditions, be sooner or later tempted to take the easy road of turning into a simple robber who preys on the poor as well as the rich (except perhaps in his native village), a retainer of the lords, a member of some strong-arm squad which comes to terms with the structures of official power. That is why the few who do not, or who are believed to have remained uncontaminated, have so great and passionate a burden of admiration and longing laid upon them. They cannot abolish oppression. But they do prove that justice is possible, that poor men need not be humble, helpless and meek.*

That is why Robin Hood cannot die, and why he is invented even when he does not really exist. Poor men have need of him, for he represents justice, without which, as Saint Augustine observed, kingdoms are nothing but great robbery. That is why they need him most, perhaps, when they cannot hope to overthrow oppression, but merely seek its alleviation, even when they half-accept the law which condemns the brigand, who yet represents divine justice and a higher form of society which is powerless to be born:

---

* It is significant that the leaders of legendary bands are often presented as personally weak or defective and are rarely supposed to be the strongest members of their band. 'For the Lord wished to prove by his example that all of us, everyone that is frightened, humble and poor, can do great deeds if God will have it so.'[20]

I the scriptures have fulfilled,
Though a wicked life I led
When the naked I beheld
I've clothed them and fed;
Sometime in a coat of winter's pride,
Sometime in russet grey,
The naked I've clothed and the hungry I've fed,
And the rich I've sent empty away.[21]

5

***

The Avengers

> God himself almost repents
> Having made the human race,
> For all is injustice,
> Affliction and vanity,
> And man, however pious,
> Cannot but regard as cruel
> The supreme Majesty.
>
> *Brazilian bandit-romance.*[1]

Ah gentlemen, if I had been able to read and write, I'd have destroyed the human race.

Michele Caruso, shepherd and bandit, captured at Benevento 1863

Moderation in killing and violence belongs to the image of the social bandits. We need not expect them as a group to live up to the moral standards they accept and their public expects from them, any more than the ordinary citizen. Nevertheless it is at first sight strange to encounter bandits who not only practise terror and cruelty to an extent which cannot possibly be explained as mere backsliding, but whose terror actually forms part of their public image. They are heroes not in spite of the fear and horror their actions inspire, but in some ways because of them. They are not so much men who right wrongs, but avengers, and exerters of power; their appeal is not that of the agents of justice – but revenge and retaliation are inseparable from justice in societies where blood calls for blood – but of men who prove that even the poor and weak can be terrible.

Whether we ought to regard these public monsters as a special sub-variety of social banditry, is not easy to say. The moral world to which they belong (i.e. which finds expression in the songs, poems and chapbooks about them) contains the values of the 'noble robber' as well as those of the monster. As the bush poet wrote of the great Lampião:

> He killed for play
> Out of pure perversity
> And gave food to the hungry
> With love and charity.

Among the *cangaçeiros* of the Brazilian north-east there are those, like the great Antonio Silvino (1875–1944, *fl.* as bandit chief 1896–1914), who are mainly remembered for their good deeds, and others, like Rio Preto, mainly for their cruelty. However, broadly speaking, the 'image' of the *cangaçeiro* combines both. Let us illustrate this by following the account of one of the backwoods bards of the most celebrated *cangaçeiro*, Virgulino Ferreira da Silva (?1898–1938), universally known as 'The Captain' or 'Lampião'.

He was born, so the legend goes (and it is the image rather than the reality which interests us for the moment), of respectable cattle-raising and farming parents at the foot of the mountains in the dry backlands of Pernambuco State 'in that time of the past when the back country was pretty prosperous', an intellectual – and therefore in the legend not a particularly powerful – boy. The weak must be able to identify with the great bandit. As the poet Zabele wrote:

> Where Lampião lives
> Worms become brave,

> The monkey fights the jaguar,
> The sheep stands his ground.

His uncle, Manoel Lopes, said this boy must become a doctor, which made people smile for

> Never was seen a doctor
> In that immense *sertão*;
> There men knew only cowhands,
> Bands of *cangaçeiros*
> Or ballad-singers.

Anyway, young Virgulino did not want to be a doctor but a *vaqueiro* or cowpuncher, though he learned his letters and the 'Roman algorism' after only three months at school and was an expert poet. The Ferreiras were expelled by the Nogueiras from their farm when he was seventeen, being falsely accused of theft. That is how the feud began which was to make him into an outlaw. 'Virgulino,' someone said, 'trust in the divine judge,' but he answered: 'The good book says honour your father and mother, and if I did not defend our name, I would lose my manhood.' So

> He bought a rifle and dagger
> In the town of São Francisco

and formed a band with his brothers and twenty-seven other fighters (known to the poet as to their neighbours by nicknames, often traditional to those who took up the career of the bandit) to attack the Nogueiras in the Serra Vermelha. From blood-feud to outlawry was a logical – in view of the superior power of the Nogueiras a necessary – step. Lampião became a roving bandit, more famous even than Antonio Silvino, whose capture in 1914 had left a void in the backwoods pantheon:

He spared the skin
Neither of soldier nor civilian,
His darling was the dagger
His gift was the gun . . .
He left the rich as beggars,
The brave fell at his feet,
While others fled the country.

But during all the years (in fact *c.* 1920–38) when he was the terror of the north-east, he never ceased to deplore his fate, says the poet, which had made him a robber instead of an honest labourer, and destined him for certain death, tolerable only if he had the luck to die in a fair fight.

He was and is a hero to the people, but an ambiguous one. Normal caution might explain why the poet makes his bow to formal morality and records the 'joy of the north' at the death of the great bandit. (By no means all ballads take this view.) The reaction of a backwoodsman in the township of Mosquito is probably more typical. When the soldiers came by with their victims' heads in jars of kerosene, so as to convince all that Lampião was really dead, he said: 'They have killed the Captain, because strong prayer is no good in water'.[2] For his last refuge was in the dried bed of a stream, and how else except by the failure of his magic could his fall be explained? Nevertheless, though a hero, he was not a *good* hero.

It is true that he had made a pilgrimage to the famous Messiah of Juazeiro, Padre Cicero, asking his blessing before turning bandit, and that the saint, though exhorting him vainly to give up the outlaw's life, had given him a document appointing him captain, and his two brothers lieutenants.[*] However, the ballad from which I have taken most of this account does not mention any righting of wrongs (except

[*] For the real basis of this story, see below pp. 100–101.

those done to the band itself), no taking from the rich to give to the poor, no bringing of justice. It records battles, and wounds, raids on towns (or what passed for towns in the Brazilian backwoods), kidnappings, hold-ups of the rich, adventures with the soldiers, with women, with hunger and thirst, but nothing that recalls the Robin Hoods. On the contrary, it records 'horrors': how Lampião murdered a prisoner though his wife had ransomed him, how he massacred labourers, tortured an old woman who cursed him (not knowing whom she entertained) by making her dance naked with a cactus bush until she died, how he sadistically killed one of his men who had offended him by making him eat a litre of salt, and similar incidents. To be terrifying and pitiless is a more important attribute of this bandit than to be the friend of the poor.

And curiously enough, though the real life Lampião was undoubtedly capricious and sometimes cruel, he saw himself as the upholder of right in at least one important respect: sexual morality.

Seducers were castrated, bandits forbidden to rape women (given the attractions of their calling, they would rarely need to), and public opinion in the band was shocked at the order to shave off a woman's hair and drive her naked away, even though she was being punished for treason. At least one member of the band, Angelo Roque, nicknamed Labarêda, who retired to become doorkeeper at the Law Courts in Bahia (! !), seems to have had the genuine instincts of a Robin Hood. Yet these characteristics do not dominate in the myth.

Terror is indeed part of the image of numerous bandits:

> All the plain of Vich
> Trembles as I pass . . .

says the hero of one of the numerous ballads celebrating the Catalan *bandoleros* of the sixteenth and seventeenth centuries, in which 'episodes of generosity do not abound' (in the words of their excellent historian Fuster), though the popular heroes among them are in most other respects 'noble'. They become *bandoleros* through some non-criminal action, rob the rich and not the poor, must remain 'honourable' as they were at the outset, e.g. kill only 'in the discharge of honour'. Terror, as we shall see, is an integral part of the image of the haiduks, who do not give much to the poor either. Once again it is mixed with some characteristics of the 'noble robber'. Terror and cruelty, again, are combined with 'nobility' in the character of an entirely fictional desperado, Joaquin Murieta, who championed Mexicans against Yankees in early California – a literary invention, but one credible enough to have entered Californian folklore and even historiography. In all these cases the bandit is essentially a symbol of power and vengeance.

The examples of genuinely unqualified cruelty, on the other hand, are not normally those of characteristic bandits. It is perhaps a mistake to classify as banditry the epidemic of blood-lust which swept the Peruvian department of Huanuco from about 1917 to the late 1920s, for though robbery formed part of it, its motive is described as 'not exactly this, but rather hatred and blood-feud'. It was indeed, according to the evidence, a blood-feud situation which got out of hand, and produced that 'fever of death among men', which led them to 'burn, rape, kill, sack and destroy coldly' everywhere except in their native community or village. Even more obviously the ghastly phenomenon of the Colombian *violencia* of the years after 1948 goes far beyond ordinary social banditry. Nowhere is the element of pathological violence for its own sake more startling than in this peasant revolution aborted into anarchy, though some of the most terrible practices, such as that of chopping prisoners into tiny fragments 'in front of and for the entertainment of the fighting men crazed by barbarity' (later to be known as *picar a tamal*) are alleged to have occurred in earlier guerrilla campaigns in that bloodthirsty country.[3] The point to note about these epidemics of cruelty and massacre is that they are immoral even by the standards of those who participate in them. If the massacre of entire bus-loads of harmless passengers or villagers is comprehensible in the context of savage civil warfare, such (well-attested) incidents as ripping the foetus out of a pregnant woman and substituting a cock can only be conscious 'sins'. And yet, some of the men who perpetrate these monstrosities are and remain 'heroes' to the local population.

Excessive violence and cruelty are thus phenomena which only overlap banditry at certain points. Nevertheless, it is sufficiently significant to require some explanation *as a social phenomenon*. (That this or that individual bandit may be a psychopath is irrelevant; in fact, it is rather improbable that many peasant bandits are psychologically deranged.)

Two possible reasons can be accepted, but are not sufficient to account for the whole of ultra-violence. The first is that, in the words of the Turkish author Yashar Kemal, 'brigands live by love and fear. When they inspire only love, it is a weakness. When they inspire only fear, they are hated and have no supporters.'[4] In other words, even the best of bandits must demonstrate that he can be 'terrible'. The second is that cruelty is inseparable from vengeance, and vengeance is an entirely legitimate activity for the noblest of bandits. To make the oppressor pay for the humiliation inflicted on the victim in his own coin is impossible; for the oppressor acts within a framework of accepted wealth, power and social superiority which the victim cannot use, unless there has been a social revolution which unseats the mighty as a class and elevates the humble. He has only his private resources and among them violence and cruelty are the most visibly effective. Thus in the well-known Bulgarian ballad of cruel banditry, 'Stoian and Nedelia', Stoian and the bandits raid the village in which he was once mistreated as Nedelia's hired servant. He kidnaps her and makes her the bandits' serving-maid, but the humiliation is not enough: he cuts off her head for revenge.

Clearly, however, there is more to the outbursts of apparently gratuitous cruelty than this. Two possible explanations may be suggested with some hesitation, for social psychology is a jungle into which only a fool ventures carelessly.

Several of the best-known examples of ultra-violence are associated with particularly humiliated and inferior groups (e.g. the coloured in societies of white racialism), or with the even more galling situation of minorities oppressed by majorities. It is perhaps no accident that the creator of the noble but also notably cruel band of Joaquin Murieta, avenger of the Californian Mexicans against the conquering *gringos*, was himself a Cherokee Indian, that is to say a member of an even more hopelessly dominated minority group. Lopez Albujar, who has described the storm of blood which swept the Indian peasants of Huanuco (Peru), has seen the connection admirably. These 'bandits' robbed, burned and murdered, at bottom 'in retaliation against the insatiable rapacity of all men who did not belong to their race', i.e. the whites. The occasional savage *jacqueries* of the Indian serfs against their white masters in Bolivia, before the revolution of 1952, show similar (temporary) shifts from the normal stolid passivity of the peasant to cruel fury.

A wild and indiscriminate retaliation: yes, but perhaps also, and especially among the weak, the permanent victims who have no hope of real victory even in their dreams, a more general 'revolution of destruction', which tumbles the whole world in ruins, since no 'good' world seems possible.

Stagolee, the mythical hero of the Negro ballad, destroys the entire city like an earthquake, another Samson. Brecht's Pirate Jenny, the lowest kitchenmaid in the sleaziest hotel, the victim of all who meet her, dreams of the pirates who will come in their eight-sailed ship, capture the city, and ask her who shall be spared. None shall be spared, they must all die, and Pirate Jenny will joke as their heads fall. Thus in the romances of the oppressed labourers of the Italian south the heroes of legend, such as the Calabrian bandit Nino Martino, dreamed of universal ruin. In such circumstances to assert power, any power, is itself a triumph. Killing and torture is the most primitive and personal assertion of ultimate power, and the weaker the rebel feels himself to be at bottom, the greater, we may suppose, the temptation to assert it.

But even when such rebels triumph, victory brings its own temptation to destroy, for primitive peasant insurgents have no positive programme, only the negative programme of getting rid of the superstructure which prevents men from living well and dealing fairly, as in the good old days. To kill, to slash, to burn away everything that is not necessary and useful to the man at the plough or with the herdsman's crook, is to abolish corruption and leave only what is good, pure and natural. Thus the brigand guerrillas of the Italian south destroyed not only their enemies and the legal documents of bondage, but unnecessary riches. Their social justice was destruction.

There is, however, another situation in which violence passes the bounds of what is conventionally accepted even in habitually violent societies. This occurs during periods of rapid social change, which destroy the traditional mechanisms of social control holding destructive anarchy at bay. The phenomenon of feuds 'getting out of hand' is familiar to observers of societies regulated by blood-vengeance. This is normally a social device containing its own automatic brake.

Once the score between two feuding families is evened, by another death or some other compensation, a settlement is negotiated, guaranteed by third parties, by intermarriage or in other well-understood ways, so that killing shall not proceed without end. Yet if for some reason (such as, most obviously, the intervention of the new-fangled state in some way incomprehensible to local custom, or by lending support to the more politically influential of the contending families) the brake ceases to function, feuds develop into those protracted mutual massacres which end either with the extirpation of one family or, after years of warfare, the return to the negotiated settlement which ought to have been made at the outset. As we have seen in the example of Lampião, such breakdowns in the customary mechanism of feud-settlement can among other things multiply outlaws and bandits (and indeed feud is the almost invariable starting-point of a Brazilian *cangaçeiro's* career).

We have some excellent examples of more general break-downs in such customary devices of social control. In his admirable autobiography *Land Without Justice*, Milovan Djilas describes the ruin of the system of values which governed the behaviour of men in his native Montenegro, after the First World War. And he records a strange episode. The Orthodox Montenegrins had always been accustomed, in addition to their internal feuding, to raid or be raided by their neighbours, the Catholic Albanians and the Moslem Bosnians. In the early 1920s a party set out to raid the Bosnian villages as men had done from time immemorial. To their own horror they discovered themselves to be doing things which raiders had never done before and which they knew to be wrong: torturing, raping, murdering children. *And they could not help themselves*. The rules men lived by had once been clearly understood; their rights and obligations, like the scope, the limits, the times and the objects of their actions, were established by custom and precedent. They were compelling not only for this reason but because they were part of a system, and one whose elements did not conflict too obviously with reality. One part of the system had broken down: they could no longer regard themselves as 'heroes' since (if we follow Djilas's argument) they had not fought to the death against the Austrian conquest. Hence the other parts ceased also to operate: when going out to fight they could no longer behave as 'heroes'. Not until the heroic system of values was restored on a new and more viable basis – paradoxically enough by the mass adhesion of the Montenegrins to the Communist Party – did the society recover its 'mental balance'. When the call for a rising against the Germans went out in 1941, thousands of men with rifles went into the Montenegrin hills to fight, kill and die 'honourably' once again.*

Banditry, we have seen, grows and becomes epidemic in times of social tension and upheaval. These are also the times when the conditions for such explosions of cruelty are most favourable. They do not belong to the central image of brigandage, except insofar as the bandit is at all times an avenger of the poor. But at such times they will no doubt occur more frequently and systematically. Nowhere more so than in those peasant insurrections and rebellions which have failed to turn into social revolutions, and whose militants are forced to fall back into the life of outlaws and robbers: hungry, embittered and resentful even against the poor who have left them to fight alone. Or, what is even worse, among that second generation of 'children of violence' who graduate from the ashes of their homes, the corpses of their fathers and the raped bodies of their mothers and sisters to the life of outlawry:

*The Montenegrins, 1.4 per cent of the Yugoslav population, provided 17 per cent of the officers in the Partisan army.

'What has impressed you most?

Seeing the houses burn.

What made you suffer most?

My mother and my little brothers weeping for hunger on the mountain.

Have you been wounded?

Five times, all rifle shots.

What would you like most?

Let them leave me in peace and I shall work. I want to learn to read.

But all they want is to kill me. I'm not one they will leave alive.'[5]

The speaker is the Colombian band chieftain Teofilo Rojas ('Chispas'), aged twenty-two and at the time of this interview charged with about four hundred crimes: thirty-seven massacred in Romerales, eighteen in Altamira, eighteen in Chili, thirty in San Juan de la China and again in El Salado, twenty-five in Toche and again in Guadual, fourteen in Los Naranjos and so on.

Monsignor German Guzman, who knows the *violencia* of his native Colombia better than most, has described these lost and murderous children of anarchy. For them:

In the first place man and land, so essentially tied together in the peasant's life, have been torn apart. They do not till the soil nor care for the trees . . . They are men, or rather adolescents, without hope. Uncertainty surrounds their lives, which find expression in adventure, self-realization in mortal undertakings, which have no transcendental meaning. Second, they have lost the sense of the farm as an anchor, a place to love, from which to draw tranquillity, a feeling of security and permanence. They are forever itinerant adventurers and vagabonds. Instability and the loosening of bonds come with outlawry. For them to halt, to grow fond of a place, would be the equivalent of giving themselves up; it would be the end. Thirdly, their rootless lives take these young enemies of society into temporary, precarious and insecure environments very different from those of the lost home. Their nomadic life implies a disordered search for the occasions of emotional satisfaction, for which they no longer have a stable framework. Here lies the key to their sexual anxiety and the pathological frequency of their aberrant crimes. For them love means most commonly rape or casual concubinage . . . When they think the girls want to leave them for any reason, they kill them. Fourthly, they lose the sense of the *path* as an element that integrates peasant life. The highlander cares for the paths along which men carry their countless loads, until in a sense they become his own intimate possession. It is a sort of love which makes men invariably come and go along them. But the anti-social bandit of our day leaves the known footpath, because the soldiers pursue him, or because guerrilla tactics compel him to seek places for unsuspected ambush or secret tracks to the surprise assault.[6]

Only a firm ideology and discipline can prevent men from degenerating into wolves under such circumstances, but neither are characteristics of the grass-roots rebel.

Still, though we must mention the pathological aberrations of banditry, the violence and cruelty which is most permanent and characteristic is the one which is inseparable from revenge. Revenge for personal humiliation, but also revenge on those who have oppressed others. In May 1744 the bandit captain Oleksa Dovbuš attacked the seat of Konstantin Zlotnicky, Gentleman. He held his hands in the fire and let them burn, poured glowing coals on his skin and refused any ransom. 'I have not come for ransom but for your soul, for you have tortured the people long enough'; so the Cistercian monks of Lwow report him. He also killed Zlotnicky's wife and half-grown son. The chronicle of the monks concludes its entry with the observation that Zlotnicky had been a cruel lord, who had in his time caused many to be killed. Where men become bandits, cruelty breeds cruelty, blood calls for blood.[7]

6

***

Haiduks

Nemtcho has become an orphan,
without father, without mother,
and on earth he has no person
to give counsel, to direct him,
how to till and how to harvest
on the land his father left him.
But instead he is a haiduk,
standard-bearer of the haiduks,
and the keeper of their treasure.

Haiduk ballad[1]

In the mountains and empty plains of south-eastern Europe the advance of Christian landlords and Turkish conquerors made life increasingly burdensome for the peasants from the fifteenth century on but, unlike more densely settled or firmly administered regions, left a broad margin of potential freedom. Groups and communities of free, armed and combative men therefore emerged among those expelled from their lands or escaping from serfdom, at first almost spontaneously, later in organized forms. What a scholar has called 'military strata sprung from the free peasantry' therefore became characteristic of this large zone, groups called Cossacks in Russia, *klephtes* in Greece, *haidamaks* in Ukraine, but in Hungary and the Balkan peninsula north of Greece mainly haiduks (*hajdú, hajdut, hajdutin*), a word probably of

Magyar origin, originally signifying 'cattle-drover'. They were a collective form of that individual peasant dissidence which, as we have seen, produced the classical bandits.

As with the men among whom Robin Hoods and avengers were recruited, haiduks were not automatically committed to rebellion against all authority. They could, as in some parts of Hungary, become attached to lords whom they provided with fighters against a recognition of their status as free men. By a natural development of reality and language the term '*heiduck*' describing the free robber-liberator *par excellence* could thus also become the term for one of the numerous types of flunkey of the German nobility. More commonly, as in Russia and Hungary, they accepted land from the emperor or Tsar or other prince against the obligation to maintain arms and horses, and to fight the Turk under chieftains of their own choosing, and thus became the guardians of the military frontier, a sort of rank-and-file knighthood. Nevertheless, they were essentially free – as such, superior to and contemptuous of servile peasants, but constant magnets to rebel and runaway elements, and with a far from unconditional loyalty. The great peasant revolts of seventeenth- and eighteenth-century Russia all began on the Cossack frontier.

There was, however, a third type of haidukdom, which refused to attach itself to any Christian noble or ruler, if only because in the area in which it flourished most nobles and rulers were unbelieving Turks. Neither royal nor signorial, these free haiduks were robbers by trade, enemies of the Turks and popular avengers by social role, primitive movements of guerrilla resistance and liberation. As such they appear in the fifteenth century, possibly first in Bosnia and Herzegovina, but later all over the Balkans and Hungary, most notably in Bulgaria, where a '*haidot*' chieftain is recorded as early as 1454. These are the men whose name I have chosen to typify the highest form of primitive banditry, the one which comes closest to being a permanent and conscious focus of peasant insurrection. Such 'haiduks' existed not only in South-Eastern Europe, but under other names in various other parts of the world, e.g. Indonesia and, most notably, Imperial China. For obvious reasons they were most common among peoples oppressed by conquerors of foreign language or religion, but not only there.

Ideology or class-consciousness was not normally the motive which drove men to become haiduks, and even the sort of non-criminal troubles which drove individual bandits into outlawry were not particularly common. We have examples of this kind, such as the Bulgarian haiduk chieftain Panayot Hitov (who has left us an invaluable autobiography), who took to the mountains at the age of twenty-five after a fight with a Turkish law official, arising out of some obscure legal trouble, in the 1850s. In general, however, if we are to believe the innumerable haiduk songs and ballads which are one of the chief sources for our knowledge of this type of banditry, the motive to become a haiduk was strictly economic. The winter was bad, says one such song, the summer was parched, the sheep died. So Stoian became a haiduk:

> Whoever wants to become a free haiduk,
> step this way, stand up beside me.
> Twenty lads thus came together,
> And we'd nothing, not a thing between us,
> no sharp swords, but only sticks.[2]

Conversely, Tatuncho the haiduk returned to the family holding because his mother pleaded with him, and anyway she said a robber could not feed his family. But the sultan sent his soldiers to capture him. He killed them all and brought the money in their belts back: 'There's the money, mother, who will say that a bandit does not feed his mother?' In fact, with luck brigandage was a better financial proposition than peasant life.

Under the circumstances, pure social banditry was rare. Panayot Hitov singles out one such rarity in his proud survey of the celebrated practitioners of the calling which he himself adorned: a certain Doncho Vatach, who flourished in the 1840s, only persecuted Turkish evildoers, helped the Bulgarian poor and distributed money. The classical 'noble robber' of Bulgaria, observed the British authors of *A Residence in Bulgaria* (1869), as so often inclined to sympathize with Islamic heroism, were the *chelibi*, normally 'well-born' Turks, as distinct from the *khersis* or ordinary robbers, who enjoyed the sympathy of their villages, and the haiduks, who were murdering outlaws, cruel by nature and unsupported except in their own band. This may be an exaggeration, but certainly the haiduks were not Robin Hoods, and their victims were anyone they could catch. The ballads are full of variations on the phrase:

> We have made many mothers weep,
> We have widowed many wives,
> Many more have we made orphans,
> For we are childless men ourselves.

Haiduk cruelty is a familiar theme. Unquestionably the haiduk was far more permanently cut off from the peasantry than the classical social bandit, not only masterless but also – at least during their bandit career – often kinless men ('without mothers all, and without sisters'), living with the peasantry not so much like Mao's proverbial fish in water, but rather like soldiers who leave their village for the semi-permanent exile of army life. A rather high proportion of them were in any case herdsmen and drovers, i.e. semi-migratory men whose links with the settlements are intermittent or tenuous. It is significant that the Greek *klephtes* (and perhaps the Slav haiduks also) had their special language or argot.

The distinction between robber and hero, between what the peasant would accept as 'good' and condemn as 'bad', was therefore exceptionally difficult, and haiduk songs insist on their sins as often as on their virtues, as the famous Chinese Water Margin novel insists on the inhumanity (expressed in the familiar anecdotes of several who eventually join the large and variegated company of the heroic out-laws).* The definition of the haiduk hero is fundamentally political. In the Balkans he was a *national* bandit, according to certain traditional rules, i.e. a defender or avenger of Christians against Turks. Insofar as he fought against the oppressor, his image was positive, though his actions might be black and his sins might lead him to eventual repentance as a monk, or punish him with nine years' illness. Unlike the 'noble robber', the haiduk does not depend on personal moral approval; unlike the 'avenger' his cruelty is not his essential characteristic, but tolerated because of his services to the people.

What made this collection of the socially marginal, the men who chose not so much freedom as against serfdom, but robbery as against poverty, into a quasi-political movement, was a powerful tradition, a recognized collective social function. As we have seen, their motives for going into the mountains were mainly economic, but the technical term for becoming a haiduk was 'to rebel', and the haiduk was by definition an insurrectionary. He joined a recognized social group. Without Robin Hood the merry men in Sherwood

---

* However, I do not know of any haiduks who are accused of the anthropophagic practices – most commonly the slaughtering of travellers whose meat is sold to butchers – which the public seems to reserve for criminals genuinely regarded as outside normal society.

Forest are insignificant, but 'the haiduks' in the Balkans, like 'the bandits' on the Chinese mountain beyond the lake, are always there to receive the dissident or the outlaw. Their chieftains change, and some of them are more celebrated or nobler than others, but neither the existence nor the fame of the haiduks depends on the reputation of any single man. To this extent they are a socially recognized collection of heroes, and indeed, so far as I can tell, the protagonists of the haiduk ballad-cycles are not the men who became famous chieftains in real life, but the anonymous – or rather those called simply Stoian or Ivantcho like any peasant; not even necessarily the leaders of bands. The klephtic ballads of Greece are both less anonymous and less socially informative, belonging as they do to the literature of the praise (and self-praise) of professional fighting men. Their heroes are almost by definition celebrated figures, known to one and all.

Permanent existence went with formal structure and organization. The organization and hierarchy of the great brigand republic which is the subject of the Chinese Water-Margin novel, is extremely elaborate; and not only because it has, unlike the illiterate lands of Europe, an honoured place for the ex-civil-servant and the displaced intellectual. (In fact, one of its main themes is the replacement of a low-grade intellectual bandit chief – one of those failed examination candidates who were so obvious a source of political dissidence in the heavenly empire – by a successful intellectual one; as it were the triumph of the first-class mind.) Haiduk bands were led by (elected) *voivodes* or dukes, whose duty was to supply arms assisted by a standard-bearer or *bairaktar*, who carried the red or green banner and also acted as treasurer and quartermaster. We find a similar military structure and terminology among the Russian *rasboiniki* and in some of the Indian dacoit communities, as among the Sansia, whose bands of *sipahis* (*sepoys*, *spahis* = soldiers) were

Dick Turpin 'as he
concealed himself
in a cave in
Epping Forest'.
Engraving by J.
Smith, 1739.

Turpin, as he conceal'd himself in a Cave on Epping Forrest.

Modern Corsican bandits. N. Romanetti (1884–1926) of Vizzanova, successor of Bellacosia as leading bandit of the island, who was killed fighting. Photographed with his elegant son (right). *Top right:* an earlier bandit wearing traditional stocking cap (Phrygian bonnet).

The bandolero romanticised by John Haynes Williams
(1836–1908), whose every picture told a Victorian story, often
about Spanish bandits and bullfighters.

Salvatore Giuliano (1922–50). The most celebrated bandit of the Italian republic was much, and flatteringly, photographed by journalists.

Lampião (?1898–1938), the great bandit-hero of Brazil. Title-page of part 1 of a three-part verse romance by a north-eastern balladeer, published in the giant industrial city of São Paulo (1962).

The bandit as national myth, propagated by intellectuals: a still from the Brazilian film *O Cangaçeiro* (1953). The decorated leather hats with upturned brim are the local equivalent of the sombrero or stetson.

The klephtic image: Giorgios Volanis (centre), leader of Greek bands in Macedonia in the early 1900s. Note the warrior's ornaments.

Balkan irregulars: Constantine Garefis, with his band (recruited around Olympus), c. 1905. He was killed by his enemies the Macedonian *Komitadjis* in 1906.

The bandit of the plains.
Sandor Rósza (1813–78),
the great Hungarian brigand-
guerilla, in jail. A band-leader
from *c.* 1841, a national
guerilla after 1849, he was
captured in 1856 and pardoned
in 1867.

Sandor Rósza as legend: a
scene from Miklos Jancso's
film *The Round-Up*, which
deals with the pursuit of
Rósza by the imperial
authorities.

Above Execution of Namoa
Pirates, Kowloon, 1891, with
British sahibs. Namoa, an
island off Swatow, was a great
centre for piracy and, at this
time, the scene of a rebellion.
We do not know whether the
corpses had been pirates,
rebels or both.

The Pindaris, described as 'a
well-known professional class
of freebooters', were
associated with the Marathas
in whose campaigns they took
part, looting. After the British
pacification the remainder
settled down as cultivators.

led by Jemadars, who received two shares of loot for every one distributed to the ranker, but also ten per cent of the total for the provision of torches, spears and other tools of the trade.*

Haiduk banditry was therefore in every respect a more serious, a more ambitious, permanent and institutionalized challenge to official authority than the scattering of Robin Hoods or other robber rebels which emerged from any normal peasant society. It is not easy to say whether this was so because certain geographical or political conditions made possible such permanent and formalized banditry, and therefore automatically made it potentially more 'political', or whether it was certain political situations (e.g. foreign conquest or certain types of social conflict) which encouraged unusually 'conscious' forms of banditry and thus structured it more firmly and permanently. Both, we may say, begging the question, though it still requires an answer. I do not think that the individual haiduk would have been able to give it, for he would rarely if ever be able to step outside the social and cultural frame which enclosed him and his people. Let us try and draw a brief portrait-sketch of him.

He would see himself, above all, as a free man – and as such as good as a lord or king; a man who had in this sense won personal emancipation and therefore superiority. The *klephtes* on Mount Olympus who captured the respectable

---

* Indian dacoits were generally classified as either 'criminal castes' or 'criminal tribes' by the British. But behind the familiar Indian penchant for giving every social and occupational group its separate social identity – i.e. what is vulgarly called the 'caste system' – we can often detect something not unlike haidukdom. Thus the most celebrated of the north Indian bandit 'tribes', the Badhaks, were originally outcasts of Moslem and Hindu provenance, 'a sort of Cave of Adullam for the reception of vagrants and bad characters of different tribes'; the Sansia, though perhaps developed from among hereditary bards and genealogists – they still held this function among some Rajputs at the end of the nineteenth century – freely accepted outside recruits into their community; and the formidable Minas of central India are supposed to have been dispossessed peasants and village watchmen who took to the hills and became professional brigands.

Herr Richter, prided themselves on their equality to kings, and rejected certain kinds of behaviour as 'un-royal', and therefore improper. Just so the north Indian Badhaks claimed that 'our profession has been a king's trade', and – at least in theory – accepted the obligations of chivalry, such as not insulting females, and killing only in fair fight, though we may regard it as certain that few haiduks could actually afford to fight in this noble manner. Freedom implied equality among haiduks and there are some impressive examples of it. For instance, when the King of Oudh tried to form a regiment of Badhaks, much as the Russian and Austrian emperors formed haiduk and Cossack units, they mutinied because the officers had refused to perform the same duties as the men. Such behaviour is unusual enough, but in a society so imbued with caste inequality as the Indian, it almost passes belief.

Haiduks were always free men, but in the typical case of the Balkan haiduks they were not free communities. For the *četa* or band, being essentially a voluntary union of individuals who cut themselves off from their kin, was automatically an abnormal social unit, since it lacked wives, children and land. It was doubly 'unnatural', for often the haiduk's road back to ordinary civilian life in his own native village was barred by the Turks. The haiduk ballads sing of the men whose swords were their only sisters, whose rifles their wives, and who would shake hands silently and sadly as the *četa* broke up, to disperse as lost individuals to the four corners of the earth. Death was their equivalent of marriage, and the ballads constantly speak of it as such. Normal forms of social organization were therefore not available to them, any more than to soldiers on campaigns, and unlike the great bands of marauding *krdžali** of the late eighteenth and early

* Troops of disbanded soldiers and desperadoes who roamed Bulgaria at the end of the eighteenth century.

nineteenth century, who carried with them male and female harems in the usual Turkish manner, the haiduks made no attempts to establish families while they were haiduks; perhaps because their units were too small to defend them. If they had any model of social organization, it was the male brotherhood or society, of which the famous Zaporozhe Cossacks are the best-known example.

This anomaly comes out clearly in their relation to women. Haiduks like all bandits had nothing whatever against them. Quite the contrary, for as a confidential report on a Macedonian *komitadji** chief observed in 1908, 'like almost all *voivodes*, he is a great lover of women'.[3] Girls – curiously enough in the ballads some seem to have been Bulgarian Jewesses – sometimes joined the haiduks and occasionally some Boyana, Yelenka or Todorka even became a *voivode*. Some returned, after a ceremonial farewell, to ordinary life and marriage:

> Penka went on to the mountains,
> On the mountain to the haiduks,
> For she wanted to bring gifts
> For her time had come to marry:
> To each soldier she gave a handkerchief,
> In each cloth a piece of gold,
> That the haiduks should remember
> When their Penka had got wed.[4]

But it seems that for the time of their haiduk life, these runaway girls were men, dressed in men's clothes, and fighting like men. The ballad tells of the girl who returned home to the woman's role, because her mother urged her, but could not stand it, put away her spindle and took up her rifle again to be a haiduk man. Just as freedom meant noble

---

* Guerrillas established by the Supreme Committee for Macedonia and Adrianople of the Macedonian revolutionaries.

status for a man, it meant male status for a woman. Conversely, in theory at least, on the mountains haiduks avoided sex with women. The klephtic ballads insist on the enormity of touching women prisoners held for ransom or other purposes, and both they and the Bulgarian outlaws held the belief that one who attacked a woman was inevitably caught, that is to say tortured and killed by the Turks. The belief is significant, even if (as we may well suspect) the outlaws fell short of it in practice.[5] In non-haiduk bands, women are known, but not common. Lampião seems to have been the only Brazilian leader who let them share the roving life; probably after he fell in love with the beautiful Maria Bonita, an affair much celebrated in the ballads. This was noted as exceptional.

Of course it might not limit them excessively, for, like the usual robber's life, the haiduk's was seasonal. 'They have a proverb', wrote an eighteenth-century German of the Dalmatian Morlacks, '*Jurwew dance, aiducki sastance*, come St George's day, up haiduks and gather round (for then robberies are made easier by the green leaves and the abundance of travellers)'.[6] The Bulgarian haiduks buried their arms on the day of the Cross on 14/27 September until St George's Day next spring. Indeed, what could haiduks do in winter when there was nobody to rob except villagers? The hardiest might take supplies into their mountain caves, but it would be more convenient to winter in some friendly village, singing heroic songs and drinking, and if the season had been poor – for how much was there to rob on the byroads of Macedonia or Herzegovina at the best of times? – they might take service with rich peasants. Or else they might return to their kin, for in some highland areas there were 'few large families which did not send some of their members among the haiduks'.[7] If the outlaws lived as strict male brotherhoods, recognizing no bonds except those of the 'true and united band of comrades', it was only for the campaigning season.

Thus they lived their wild, free lives in the forest, the mountain caves, or on the wide steppes, armed with the 'rifle as tall as a man', the pair of pistols at the belt, the *yatagan*[*] and 'sharp Frankish sword', their tunics laced, gilded and criss-crossed by bandoleers, their moustaches bristling, conscious that fame was their reward among enemies and friends. The mythology of heroism, the ritualization of the ballad, turned them into type-figures. We know little or nothing about Novak and his sons Grujo and Radivoj, about Mihat the herdsman, Rado of Sokol, Bujadin, Ivan Visnic and Luka Golowran except that they were celebrated Bosnian haiduks of the nineteenth century, because those who sang about them (including themselves) did not have to tell their public what the lives of Bosnian peasants and herdsmen were like. Only occasionally does the cloud of heroic anonymity lift, and a haiduk career emerge at least partly into the light of history.

Such a one is that of the *voivode* Korčo, the son of a shepherd from near Strumica (in Macedonia), who served a Turkish Beg. An epidemic killed the flock, and the Beg imprisoned the father. The son went into the mountains to threaten the Turk, but in vain: the old man died in jail. At the head of a haiduk band Korčo then captured a young Turkish 'nobleman', broke his arms and legs, cut off his head and paraded it through the Christian villages on a lance. After that he was a haiduk for ten years, until he bought some mules, exchanged haiduk costume for the merchant's and vanished – at least from the world of heroic memories – for another ten. At the end of this time he appeared at the head of three hundred men (let us not inquire too closely into the rounded

[*]Mohammedan sword without guard to handle, often with a double-curved blade.

numbers of epics) and took service with the redoubtable Pasvan (Osman Pasvanoglu, a Mohammedan Bosnian who became Pasha of Vidin), who was in opposition to the Sublime Porte and led the savage formations of *krdžali* against the Sultan's more loyal servants. Korčo did not stay long in the service of Pasvan. Setting off on his own again he attacked and captured the town of Strumica, not only because peasant haiduks hated and distrusted cities, but because it sheltered the Beg who had caused his father's death. He killed the Beg and massacred the population. Then he returned to Vidin and history or legend loses track of him. His end is unknown. Since the era of the *krdžali* raids was, approximately, the 1790s and 1800s, his career can be roughly dated. His story is told by Panayot Hitov.

Their existence was its own justification. It proved that oppression was not universal, and vengeance for oppression was possible. Hence the peasants and herdsmen in the haiduks' own home region identified with them. We need not suppose that they spent all their time fighting, let alone trying to overthrow, the oppressors. The very existence of bands of free men, or of those small patches of rock or reed beyond the reach of any administration, was sufficient achievement. Those Greek mountains proudly called Agrapha (the 'unwritten', because nobody had ever succeeded in enrolling their population for taxes) were independent in practice if not in law. So haiduks would raid. In the nature of their trade they would have to fight Turks (or whoever else represented authority), because it was authority's business to protect travelling goods and treasure. They would no doubt kill Turks with especial satisfaction, since they were unbelieving dogs and oppressors of good Christians, and perhaps also because fighting men are more heroic when they fight dangerous adversaries, whose bravery enhances their own. However, left to themselves there is no evidence that, say, the Balkan haiduks set out to liberate their land from the Turkish yoke, or would have been capable of doing so.

Of course in times of trouble for the people and crisis for authority, the number of haiduks and haiduk bands would grow, their actions multiply and become more daring. At such times the government orders to stamp out banditry would grow more peremptory, the excuses of local administrators more shrill and heartfelt, and the mood of the people tense. For, unlike the epidemics of ordinary banditry which we retrospectively discover to be forerunners of revolution only because in fact they have preceded it, haiduks were not merely symptoms of unrest but nuclei of potential liberators, recognized by the people as such. If the times were ripe, the 'liberated area' of the Chinese bandits on some mountain of Liang Shan P'o (locus of their 'lair' in the well-known Water-Margin novel) would expand to become a region, a province, the nucleus of a force to topple the throne of heaven. The roving bands of outlaws, raiders and Cossacks on the turbulent frontier between state and serfdom on one hand, the open spaces and freedom on the other, would coalesce to inspire and lead the gigantic peasant risings surging upwards along the Volga, headed by a Cossack peoples' pretender, or champion of the true Tsar against the false. Javanese peasants would listen with heightened interest to the story of Ken Angrok, the robber who became the founder of the princely house of Modjopait. If the signs are auspicious, the hundred days during which the maize ripens are past, the time is right, perhaps the millennium of freedom, always latent, always expected, is about to begin. Banditry merges with peasant revolt or revolution. The haiduks, brilliant in their tunics, formidable in their arms and accoutrements, may be its soldiers.

However, before we can consider the bandit's role in

peasant revolution, we must look at the economic and political factors which maintain him within the framework of existing society.

7

***

The Economics and Politics of Banditry

Curious enough, results of a continuous observation and inquiry coincide in this fact: That all bandits are propertyless and they are unemployed. What they may possess is personal and comes only with the success of their reckless adventure.

'An economic interpretation of the increase of bandits in China.'[1]

The robber band is outside the social order which fetters the poor, a brotherhood of the free, not a community of the subject. Nevertheless, it cannot opt out of society. Its needs and activities, its very existence, bring it into relations with the ordinary economic, social and political system. This aspect of brigandage is normally neglected by observers, but it is sufficiently important to require a little discussion.

Let us consider first the economics of banditry. Robbers must eat, and supply themselves with arms and ammunition. They must spend the money they rob, or sell their booty. It is true that in the simplest of cases they require very little other than what the local peasantry or herdsmen consume – locally produced food, drink and clothing – and may be content if they can get it in ample quantities without the ordinary man's labour. 'Nobody ever refuses them anything,' said a Brazilian landowner. 'It would be stupid to. People give them food, clothes, cigarettes, alcohol. What would they need money for? What would they do with it? Bribe the police, that's all.'[2] However, most bandits we know of live in a monetary economy, even if the surrounding peasantry does not. Where and how do they get their 'coats with the five rows of gold-plated buttons', their guns, pistols and bandoleers, the legendary 'damascene swords with the gilded handle' about which Servian haiduks and Greek *klephtes* bragged, not always with considerable exaggeration?[*]

What do they do with the rustled cattle, the travelling merchant's goods? They buy and sell. Indeed, since they normally possess far more cash than ordinary local peasantry, their expenditures may form an important element in the modern sector of the local economy, being redistributed, through local shopkeepers, innkeepers and others, to the

---

[*] The following is the police inventory of the bandit Lampião's equipment (Bahia, Brazil, 1938):

Hat: leather, of the backwoods type, decorated with six stars of Solomon. Leather chinstrap, 46 cm long, decorated with 50 gold trinkets of miscellaneous origin, to wit: collar and sleeve studs, rectangles engraved with the words Memory, Friendship, Homesickness, etc; rings set with various precious stones; a wedding ring with the name Santinha engraved inside. Attached to the front of the hat, a strip of leather 4 by 22 cm with the following ornaments: 2 gold medallions inscribed 'The Lord Be Thy Guide'; 2 gold sovereigns; 1 old Brazilian gold piece with the effigy of the Emperor Pedro II; 2 others, even older, dates respectively 1776 and 1802. At the back of the hat, a strip of leather of equal size, also decorated as follows: 2 gold medallions, 1 small diamond cut in the classic fashion, 4 others of fancy cut.

Gun: Brazilian army Mauser, model 1908, no. 314 series B. The bandoleer is decorated with 7 silver crowns of imperial Brazilian coinage and 5 discs of white metal. Safety catch is broken and reinforced with a piece of aluminium.

Knife: steel, length 67 cm. The handle is decorated with 3 gold rings. The blade has bullet-marks. Sheath nickle-plated leather, also with bullet-hole.

Cartridge-pouch: leather, ornamental. Can contain 121 rounds for Mauser or musket. A whistle is attached by a silver chain. Bullet-hole on left side.

Haversacks: 2, copiously embroidered. The embroideries are in vivid colours and done very tastefully. One is closed by means of three buttons, 2 gold, 1 silver; the other has only 1 silver button. On the carrying-straps, 9 buttons in massive silver.

Neckerchief: red silk, embroidered.

Pistol: Parabellum no. 97, 1918 model, holster, varnished black, very worn.

Sandals: one pair, of the same type as habitually worn in the *sertão*, but of excellent quality and finish.

Tunic: Blue, with three officer's stripes on the sleeves.

Blankets: 2, printed calico, lined with cotton.[3]

commercial middle strata of rural society; all the more effectively redistributed since bandits (unlike the gentry) spend most of their cash locally, and are in any case too proud and too freehanded to bargain. 'The trader sells his goods to Lampião at three times the usual price', it was said in 1930.

All this means that bandits need middlemen, who link them not only to the rest of the local economy but to the larger networks of commerce. Like Pancho Villa, they must have at least one friendly hacienda across the mountain which will take, or arrange to sell, livestock without asking awkward questions. Like the semi-nomads of Tunisia, they may institutionalize arrangements to return stolen cattle against a 'reward', through sedentary middlemen, village innkeepers or dealers who approach the victim to explain, in terms perfectly understood by all concerned, with the news that they know someone who has 'found' the strayed beasts and only wishes their owner to have them back again. Like so many of the Indian dacoit groups, they may raise the money to finance their more ambitious expeditions from money-lenders and traders in their home-base, or even rob some rich caravan virtually on commission for the entrepreneurs who have indicated it to them. For where bandits specialize in robbing transient traffic – as all sensible ones do if they have the luck to live within reach of major routes of trade and communication – they need information about forthcoming shipments or convoys, and they cannot possibly do without some mechanism for selling the loot, which may well consist of commodities for which there is no local demand.

Intermediaries are evidently also necessary for kidnappers who demand ransom, which has long been, and remains, the most lucrative source of income for bandits. Ransom is likely to be paid in cash or its equivalent, that is to say it forms part of the wider monetary economy. In China it was so common that it could be described as 'a sort of unofficial wealth tax on local property-owners', and as such socially justified in the eyes of the poor, at least so long as it was confined to the rich. As for these, since it is in the programme of every wealthy Chinese to be kidnapped sooner or later, there is always a certain sum of money laid aside to be used for ransom.'[4]

It is therefore a mistake to think of bandits as mere children of nature roasting stags in the greenwood. A successful brigand chief is at least as closely in touch with the market and the wider economic universe as a small landowner or prosperous farmer. Indeed, in economically backward regions his trade may draw him close to that of others who travel, buy and sell. The Balkan cattle- or pig-dealers may well have doubled as bandit leaders, just as merchant captains in pre-industrial days might well dabble in a little piracy (or the other way round), even when not using the good offices of governments to turn themselves into privateers, i.e. legitimate pirates. The history of Balkan liberation is familiar with heroic livestock-dealers with a reputation as band-leaders, such as Black George in Serbia or Kolokotrones in Greece; and the history of Balkan banditry is, as we have seen, not unfamiliar with haiduks who 'put on merchant's garb' for a spell and engage in trade. We tend to be amazed at the transformation of rural toughs in Corsica or inland Sicily into the *Mafiosi* businessmen and entrepreneurs who can recognize the economic opportunities of the international drug-traffic or the construction of luxury hotels as well as the next man, but the cattle-rustling on which so many of them cut their teeth is an activity which widens a peasant's economic horizon. At the very least it tends to put men in touch with those whose horizons are wider than his.

Still, economically speaking the bandit is not a very interesting figure, and though he might well deserve a footnote or two in textbooks of economic development, he probably deserves no more than this. He contributes to the accumulation of local capital – almost certainly in the hands of his parasites rather than in his own free-spending ones. Where he robs transit trade, his economic effect may be analogous to tourist travel, which also extracts income from foreigners: in this sense the brigands of the Sardinian mountains and the developers of the Aga Khan's Costa Smeralda may be economically analogous phenomena.* And that is about all. The real significance of the bandit's economic relationships is therefore different. It lies in the illumination it sheds on his situation within the rural society.

For the crucial fact about the bandit's social situation is its ambiguity. He is an outsider and a rebel, a poor man who refuses to accept the normal roles of poverty, and establishes his freedom by means of the only resources within reach of the poor – strength, bravery, cunning and determination. This draws him close to the poor: he is one of them. It sets him in opposition to the hierarchy of power, wealth and influence: he is not one of them. Nothing will make a peasant brigand into a 'gentleman', for in the societies in which bandits flourish the nobility and gentry are not recruited from the ranks. At the same time the bandit is, inevitably, drawn into the web of wealth and power, because, unlike other peasants, he acquires wealth and exerts power. He is 'one of us' who is constantly in the process of becoming associated with 'them'. The more successful he is as a bandit, the more he is *both* a representative

* Analogous even in the marginality of their effect on the surrounding economy. For where there is a particularly wide gap between the local economy and the tourist enclaves, much of the income brought in by tourists flows out again to pay for their own consumption of, e.g., luxury motor-boats, champagne and water-skis, which have also to be bought in foreign currency. Just so a brigand chief who robs merchants passing through his region, and buys jewellery, ammunition and conspicuously ornamented swords with the proceeds, or spends these on high living in the capital, is making only a marginal contribution to the income of his region.

and champion of the poor *and* a part of the system of the rich.

It is true that the isolation of rural society, the slenderness and intermittency of its relationships, the distances over which they operate, and the general primitivism of rural life, allow the bandit to keep his roles apart with some success. His equivalent in the tightly packed immigrant city slums, the local gangster or political boss (who also, in a sense, stands for the poor against the rich, and sometimes gives to the poor some of his loot from the rich), is much less the rebel and outlaw, much more the boss. His connection with the centres of official wealth and power (e.g. 'City Hall') are much more evident – they may indeed be the most evident thing about him. The rural bandit may be ostensibly quite outside the 'system'. His personal connection with the non-bandit world may be simply that of kinship, of member-ship in his local village community, that is to say he may apparently belong entirely to the independent sub-world in which peasants live, and into which the gentry, the govern-ment, the police, the tax-collectors, the foreign occupiers, only make periodic incursions. Alternatively, as the leader of a free and mobile armed band which depends on nobody, his relations with the centres of wealth and power may appear to be simply those of one sovereign body with others which affect his standing no more than trade negotiations with Britain affect the revolutionary status of Castro's Cuba. And yet, the bandit cannot escape the logic of living in a society of rule and exploitation so easily.

For the basic fact of banditry is that, quite apart from the bandit's need of business contacts, he forms a nucleus of armed strength, and therefore a political force. In the first place, a band is something with which the local system has to come to terms. Where there is no regular or effective machinery for the maintenance of public order – and this is almost by definition the case where banditry flourishes – there is not much point in appealing to the authorities for protection, all the less so as such an appeal will quite likely bring along an expeditionary force of troops, who will lay waste the countryside far more surely than the local bandits:

I much prefer dealing with bandits than with the police [said a Brazilian landowner around 1930]. The police are a bunch of 'dog-killers' who come from the capital with the idea that all the backwoodsmen protect bandits. They think we know all their escape-routes. So their chief object is to get confessions at all costs . . . If we say we don't know, they beat us. If we tell them, they still beat us, because that proves that we have been tied up with the bandits . . . The backwoodsman can't win . . . – And the bandits? – Ah, the bandits behave like bandits. Mind you, you have to know how to handle them so that they don't cause trouble. Still, leaving aside a few of the lads who really are cruel, they cause no harm except when the police is on their tails.[5]

Isolated estates in such regions have long learned how to establish diplomatic relations with brigands. Ladies of good birth recall in their memoirs how, when still children, they were hustled out of the way as some troop of armed men arrived at the *hacienda* at nightfall, to be welcomed politely and with offers of hospitality by the head of the house, and to be sent on its mysterious way with equal politeness and assurances of mutual respect. What else could he be expected to do?

Everybody has to come to terms with large and well-established bandits. This means that they are to some extent integrated into established society. The ideal is of course the formal conversion of poachers into gamekeepers, which is by no means uncommon. Cossacks are given land and privileges by lords or Tsar, in order to exchange freebooting for the protection of their lord's territory and interests. Gajraj, a chief of the Badhak dacoits, 'risen from the profession of a monkey-showman to be the Robin Hood of Gwalior' in the 1830s, 'had made himself so formidable that the Durbar appointed him to keep the *ghats* or ferries over the Chambal, which he did in a very profitable manner to them'. The Minas, another famous 'robber tribe' in central India, were the terror of Alwar, but in Jaipur they received lands rent-free in return for the duty of escorting convoys of treasure, and were celebrated for their loyalty to the Raja. In India as in Sicily the professions of village and field, or cattle-watchmen, were often interchangeable with that of bandit. The Ramosi, a small dacoit community in Bombay Presi-dency, were given land, various other perquisites and the right to charge a fee from all travellers in return for guarding the villages. What better safeguard against uncontrolled brigandage than such arrangements?[6]

Whether such arrangements are formalized or not, the inhabitants of bandit-ridden areas often have no other option. Local officials who want to carry out their jobs quietly and without fuss – as which of them do not? – will keep in touch and on reasonable terms with them, or else risk those painful local incidents which give such unwel-come publicity to a district, and cause superior officials to take a poor view of their subordinates. This explains why in really bandit-infested areas campaigns against banditry are so often carried out by special forces brought in from the outside. Local merchants make their own arrangements to safeguard their businesses against constant disruption. Even the locally stationed soldiery and police may merely prefer to keep crime – by tacit or overt agreement with the bandits – below the threshold which will attract the attention of the capital, which leaves plenty of room for banditry, for in the pre-industrial period the eye of central governments does not penetrate too deeply into the undergrowth of rural society, unless its own special interests are involved.

However, not only must local men of wealth or authority come to terms with bandits, but in many rural societies they also have a distinct interest in doing so. The politics of areas ruled by pre-capitalist landowners turn on the rivalries and relationships of the leading landed families and their respective followers and clients. The power and influence of the head of such a family rests, in the last analysis, on the number of men to whom he is patron, offering protection and receiving in turn those services of loyalty and dependence which are the measure of his prestige, and consequently of his capacity to make alliances: fighting, voting, or whatever else determines local power. The more backward the area, the more remote, weak or uninterested the higher authorities, the more vital in local politics – or for that matter as regards local influence in national politics – is this capacity of a magnate or gentleman to mobilize 'his' people. If he counts enough swords, guns or votes in the calculus of local politics, he need not even be very rich, as wealth is reckoned in prosperous and economically advanced regions. Of course wealth helps to gain a larger clientele, though only wealth freely, indeed ostentatiously, distributed to demonstrate a nobleman's status and power of patronage. On the other hand, a large and formidable following will do more to get a man estates and money than a sound head for figures; though of course the object of such politics is to accumulate not capital but family influence. Indeed, once the pursuit of wealth becomes separable from that of family interest and is superior to it, this kind of politics breaks down.

This is a situation which is ideally suited to banditry. It provides a natural demand and political role for bandits, a local reservoir of uncommitted armed men who, if they can be induced to accept the patronage of some gentleman or magnate, will greatly add to his prestige and may well on a suitable occasion add to his fighting or vote-getting force. (What is more, the establishments of retainers kept by noblemen provide convenient employment for individual bandits, potential or actual.) A wise brigand chief will take care to attach himself only to the dominant local faction, which can guarantee real protection, but even if he does not accept patronage, he can be fairly certain that most local bosses will treat him as a potential ally, and consequently a man to stay on good terms with. This is why in areas remote from effective central authority, like the back country of north-east Brazil until 1940, celebrated bands can flourish for surprisingly long periods: Lampião lasted nearly twenty years. But then Lampião had used such a political situation to build up so strong a force as to constitute not merely a potential reinforcement for any great 'colonel' of the back-woods, but a power in his own right.

In 1926 the Prestes column, a flying guerrilla formation led by a rebellious army officer who was in the process of turning himself into the leader of the Brazilian Communist Party, reached the north-east after two years of mobile operations in other parts of the interior. The Federal Government appealed for help to the Messiah of Juazeiro, Padre Cicero, whose influence had made him the effective political boss of the state of Ceará, partly because a Messiah might help to keep the faithful immune to the social-revolutionary appeals of Prestes and his men. Padre Cicero, who was far from enthusiastic about the presence of federal troops in his fief (he pointed out that his flock was unprepared to oppose anyone whom the government chose to call 'bandits', and the Prestes column did not strike the faithful as anti-social at all), accepted the suggested solution. Lampião was invited to the Father's Jerusalem, the town of Juazeiro, received with all honours, given an official rank as captain by the most senior federal official in residence (an inspector of the ministry of agriculture), together with a rifle and 300 rounds for each of his men, and told to harry the rebels.* The great bandit was immensely excited about this sudden conversion to legitimate status. However, he was advised by a friendly 'colonel' that he was merely making himself a cat's-paw of the government, which would certainly claim, once Prestes had gone, that his commission was invalid, and would equally certainly refuse to honour the promise of indemnity for past crimes. This reasoning seems to have convinced Lampião, who promptly gave up his pursuit of Prestes. No doubt he shared the general feeling of all in the backwoods that roving bands of armed men were something one knew how to deal with, but the government was both more incalculable and more dangerous.

The only bandits unable to benefit from so favourable a political situation were those with a reputation for social rebelliousness so marked that any landowner and nobleman would prefer to see them dead. There were never more than a handful of such bands, and their number was kept tiny by the very ease with which peasant bandits could establish relations with men of substance and standing.

Furthermore, the structure of politics in such rural societies provided another, and perhaps an even more formidable, reinforcement to banditry. For if the dominant families or faction protected them, the defeated or opposition groups had no recourse except to arms, which meant in extreme cases, to become band-leaders. There are innumerable examples of this. Sleeman in his *Journey through the Kingdom of Oude in 1849–50* gives a list of several, such as Imam Buksh, who still kept up his band and his plundering 'though restored to his estate on his own terms'. The practice

---

* This incident is the foundation for the passage in the romances about Lampião mentioned above.[7]

was usual, if not inevitable, in Java. A good example of such a situation was that of the department of Cajamarca in Peru in the early twentieth century which produced a number of 'opposition' bandits, notably Eleodoro Benel Zuloeta, against whom some rather elaborate military campaigns were mounted in the middle 1920s.[8] In 1914 Benel, a landowner, had leased the *hacienda* Llaucán, making himself rather unpopular with the local Indian peasantry whose discontent was mobilized against him by the brothers Ramos, who already held the sub-lease of the estate. Benel appealed to the authorities, who massacred the Indians in the usual manner of the times, thus confirming those left in their hostility. The Ramos then felt in a position to finish off Benel, but only managed to kill his son. 'Unfortunately justice failed to act and the crime remained unpunished,' as the historian tactfully puts it, adding that the assassins happened to enjoy the support of some other personal enemies of Benel, e.g. Alvarado of Santa Cruz. Thereupon Benel realized his assets to finance 'a formidable legion of his dependents (*trabaja-dores*), determined to give their lives in the service of their chief', and moved against Alvarado and the Ramos. This time justice did act, but Benel had fortified his own *hacienda* and defied it. This naturally helped him 'to win further sympathizers whom he supplied with all the necessities of life'.

He was merely the most formidable of a large number of band-leaders who emerged with the virtual breakdown of government authority, in a complex combination of political and personal rivalries, vengeance, political and economic ambition, and social rebellion. As the (military) historian of the campaign puts it:

The peasantry of those settlements was humble and sluggish, incapable of standing up against the little local tyrants. However, to feel alive is to feel rage against injustice. Hence persons of local power and authorities who lacked the intellectual preparation for their difficult duties, managed to unite a now emboldened and determined people against them . . . The history of all peoples shows that in such situations armed bands are formed. In Chota they went with Benel, in Cutervo with the Vasquez* and others. These men exercised their kind of justice, punishing those who usurped other men's land, formalizing marriages, pursuing criminals and imposing order on the local lords.

At times of elections Congressional Deputies made use of these fighters, supplying them with arms and instructing them to take action against their political adversaries. The armed hosts grew stronger and banditry reached the point at which it caused panic among the peaceful citizenry.[10]

Benel flourished until in 1923 he made the mistake of allying with some local potentates who planned to over-throw the formidable President Leguía, after which sub-stantial forces were brought into the field and the Cajamarca situation was cleared up, not without considerable efforts. He was finally killed in 1927. The Ramos and Alvarado also disappeared from the scene, together with various other band-leaders.

Such local rivalries are inseparable from banditry. The case of the Clan Macgregor in the sixteenth to eighteenth centuries, and in particular of their most famous member, Rob Roy, is very much in point. For the Macgregors remained a clan of robbers because their enemies left them no other choice but extirpation. (They were indeed form-ally dissolved and their name forbidden.) Rob Roy's own

---

* The three brothers Vasquez, Avelino, Rosendo and Paulino, were, it seems, smallholders who managed in the course of their activities to become lords of the *haciendas* of Pallac and Camsa. They were tricked into a false 'treaty of peace' and killed at the banquet organized by the sub-prefect to celebrate it.[9]

reputation as a Scottish Robin Hood derives mainly from the fact that he attacked the Duke of Montrose, the successful magnate who had, he felt, done him an injustice. In this way the armed resistance of the 'outs' to the 'ins' of local aristocratic or family politics, may, at least locally and temporarily, satisfy the resentments of the poor against their exploiters, a situation not unknown in other kinds of politics. In any case, where landowning families fight and feud, make and break family alliances, dispute heritages with arms, the stronger accumulating wealth and influence over the broken bones of the weaker, the scope for bands of fighting men led by the disgruntled losers is naturally very large.

The structure of rural politics in the conditions which breed banditry therefore has two effects. On the one hand it fosters, protects and multiplies bandits, on the other it integrates them into the political system. Admittedly both these effects are probably more powerful where the central state apparatus is absent or ineffective and the regional centres of power are balanced or unstable, as in conditions of 'feudal anarchy', in frontier zones, among a shifting mosaic of petty principalities, in the wild back country. A strong emperor, king or even baron establishes his own law on his own lands and hangs freelance bands of armed robbers instead of patronizing them, whether they threaten the social order or merely disrupt trade and disturb property. The British raj scarcely needed to recruit dacoits as escorts for its treasure-transports like the rajas of Jaipur. And men whose power is based on the generation of wealth by wealth, and who do not need (or no longer need) to accumulate wealth by the knife or gun, hire policemen to protect it rather than gangsters. The 'robber barons' of the wild era in American capitalism made the fortunes of the Pinkertons, not of freelance gunmen. It was small and weak business, labour or municipal politics which *had* to negotiate with the mobs, not big business. What is more, with economic development the rich and powerful are increasingly likely to see bandits as threats to property to be stamped out, rather than as one factor among others in the power-game.

Under such circumstances bandits become permanent outcasts, their hand against every 'respectable' man. Perhaps at this stage the anti-mythology of banditry makes its appearance, in which the robber appears as the opposite of the hero, as – to use the terminology of Russian nobles at the end of the eighteenth century – 'a beast in human form', 'ready to profane all that is holy, to kill, to pillage, to burn, to violate the will of God and the laws of the State'.[11] (It seems certain that, in Russia at least, this myth of the bandit as the negation of humanity arose considerably later than the heroic myth of folk-song and folk-epic.) The mechanism for integrating banditry into normal political life disappears. The robber now belongs only to one part of society, the poor and oppressed. He can either merge with the rebellion of peasant against lord, of traditional society against modernity, of marginal or minority communities against their integration into a wider polity, or with that permanent pendant to the 'straight' or respectable world, the 'bent' or underworld.* But even this now provides less scope for the life of the mountain, the greenwood, and the open highway. Bonnie and Clyde, the heirs of Jesse James, were not typical criminals of the American 1930s, but historical throwbacks. The nearest the really modern strong-arm man gets to the rural life is a barbecue on a country estate gained by urban crime.

---

* In exceptional cases, as in Sicily and the immigrant ghettoes of the USA, he may also merge with a new bourgeoisie.

8

***

Bandits and Revolutions

Flagellum Dei et commissarius missus a Deo contra usurarios et detinentes pecunias otiosas. (Scourge of God and envoy of God against usurers and the possessors of unproductive wealth.)

Self-description by Marco Sciarra, Neapolitan brigand chief of the 1590s.[1]

At this point the bandit has to choose between becoming a criminal or a revolutionary. As we have seen, social banditry by its nature challenges the established order of class society and political role in principle, whatever its accommodations with both in practice. Insofar as it is a phenomenon of social protest, it can be seen as a precursor or potential incubator of revolt.

In this it differs sharply from the ordinary underworld of crime, with which we have already had occasion to contrast it. The underworld (as its name implies) is an anti-society, which exists by reversing the values of the 'straight' world – it is, in its own phrase, 'bent' – but is otherwise parasitic on it. A revolutionary world is also a 'straight' world, except perhaps at especially apocalyptic moments when even the anti-social criminals have their access of patriotism or revolutionary exaltation. Hence, for the genuine underworld, revolutions are little more than unusually good occasions for crime. There is no evidence that the flourishing underworld of Paris provided revolutionary militants or sympathizers in the French revolutions of the eighteenth and nineteenth centuries, though in 1871 the prostitutes were strongly Communard; but as a class they were victims of exploitation rather than criminals. The criminal bandit gangs which infested the French and Rhineland countryside in the 1790s were not revolutionary phenomena, but symptoms of social disorder. The underworld enters the history of revolutions only insofar as the *classes dangereuses* are mixed up with the *classes laborieuses*, mainly in certain quarters of the cities, and because rebels and insurgents are often treated by the authorities as criminals and outlaws, but in principle the distinction is clear.

Bandits, on the other hand, share the values and aspirations of the peasant world, and as outlaws and rebels are usually sensitive to its revolutionary surges. As men who have already won their freedom they may normally be contemptuous of the inert and passive mass, but in epochs of revolution this passivity disappears. Large numbers of peasants *become bandits*. In the Ukrainian risings of the sixteenth and seventeenth centuries they would declare themselves Cossacks. In 1860–1 the peasant guerrilla units were formed around, and like, brigand bands: local leaders would find themselves attracting a massive influx of disbanded Bourbon soldiers, deserters, or evaders of military service, escaped prisoners, men who feared persecution for acts of social protest during Garibaldi's liberation, peasants and mountain men seeking freedom, vengeance, loot, or a combination of all these. Like the usual outlaw band, these units would initially tend to form in the neighbourhood of the settlements from which they drew their recruits, establish a base in the nearby mountains or forests, and begin their operations by activities hard to distinguish from those of ordinary bandits. Only the social setting was now different. The minority of the unsubmissive were now joined in mobilization by the majority. In short, to quote a Dutch student of Indonesia, at such times 'the robber band associates itself with other groups and expresses itself under that guise, whilst the groups which originated with more honest ideals take on the character of bandits'.[2]

An Austrian official in the Turkish service has given an excellent description of the early stages of such a peasant mobilization in Bosnia. At first it only looked like an unusually stubborn dispute about tithes. Then the Christian peasants of Lukovac and other villages gathered, left their houses and went on to the mountain of the Trusina Planina, while those of Gabela and Ravno stopped work and held meetings. While negotiations went on, a band of armed Christians attacked a caravan from Mostar near Nevesinye, killing seven Moslem carters. The Turks thereupon broke off talks. At this point the peasants of Nevesinye all took arms, went on to the mountain and lit alarm-fires. Those of Ravno and Gabela also took arms. It was evident that a major uprising was about to break out – in fact the rising which was to initiate the Balkan wars of the 1870s, to detach Bosnia and Herzegovina from the Ottoman Empire, and to have a variety of important international consequences, which do not concern us here.[3] What does concern us is the characteristic combination of mass mobilization and expanded bandit activity in such a peasant revolution.

Where there is a strong haiduk tradition or powerful independent communities of armed outlaws, free and armed peasant raiders, banditry may impose an even more distinct pattern on such revolts, since it may have already been recognized, in a vague sense, as the relic of ancient or the nucleus of future freedom. Thus in Saharanpur (Uttar Pradesh, India), the Gujars, an important minority of the population, had a strong tradition of independence or 'turbulence' and 'lawlessness' (to use the phraseology of the

British officials). The great Landhaura estate of the Gujars was broken up in 1813. Eleven years later, when times in the countryside were hard, 'the bolder spirits' in Saharanpur 'sooner than starve, banded themselves together under a brigand chief named Kallua', a local Gujar, and engaged in banditry on either side of the Ganges, robbing *banias* (the trading and moneylending caste), travellers and inhabitants of Dehra Dun. 'The motives of the dacoits', observes the Gazetteer, 'were perhaps not so much mere plunder as the desire of the return to the old lawless way of living, unencumbered by the regulations of superior authority. In short, the presence of armed bands implied rebellion rather than mere law-breaking.'[4]

Kallua, allying with an important *taluqdar*[*] who controlled forty villages and other disgruntled gentry, soon extended his revolt by attacking police posts, capturing some treasure from two hundred police guards and sacking the town of Bhagwanpur. Thereupon he declared himself to be the Raja Kalyan Singh and dispatched messengers in royal fashion to exact tribute. He now had a thousand men, and announced that he would overthrow the foreign yoke. He was defeated by a force of two hundred Gurkhas, having had 'the incredible presumption to await the attack outside the fort'. The rebellion lasted into the next year ('another hard season . . . had given them an accession of new recruits'), and then petered out.

The bandit chief who is regarded as a royal pretender or seeks to legitimize revolution by adopting the formal status of a ruler, is familiar enough. The most formidable examples are perhaps the bandit and Cossack chieftains of Russia, where the great *rasboiniki* always tended to be regarded as miraculous heroes, akin to the champions of the Holy Russian land

---

[*] Holder of hereditary estates or officer in charge of a *taluq* (district) in parts of India.

against the Tatars, if not actually as possible avatars of the
'beggars' Tsar' – the good Tsar who knew the people and
would replace the evil Tsar of the *boyars*[*] and the gentry. The
great peasant rebels of the seventeenth and eighteenth
centuries along the lower Volga were Cossacks – Bulavin,
Bolotnikov, Stenka Razin (the hero of folk-song) and
Yemelyan Pugachov – and Cossacks were in those days
communities of free peasant raiders. Like Raja Kalyan Singh,
we find them issuing imperial proclamations; like the
brigands of southern Italy in the 1860s we find their men
killing, burning, pillaging, destroying the written documents
which signify serfdom and subjection, but lacking any
programme except that of sweeping away the machinery of
oppression.

For banditry itself thus to become the revolutionary
movement and to dominate it, is unusual. As we have seen
(above, pp. 28–30), limitations, both technical and ideological, are such as to make it unsuitable for more than
momentary operations of more than a few dozen men, and its
internal organization provides no model which can be
generalized to be that of an entire society. Even the Cossacks,
who developed quite large and structured permanent communities of their own, and very substantial mobilizations for
their raiding campaigns, provided only leaders and not
models for the great peasant insurrections: it was as 'people's
Tsars' and not as *atamans*[†] that they mobilized these. Banditry
is therefore more likely to come into peasant revolutions as
one aspect of a multiple mobilization, and knowing itself to
be a subordinate aspect, except in one sense: it provides
fighting men and fighting leaders. Before the revolution it
may be, to use the phrase of an able historian of Indonesian
peasant unrest, 'a crucible out of which emerged a religious

[*] Privileged class of high nobles in Russia.
[†] Elected Cossack chieftains.

revival on one hand, and revolt on the other'.[5] As the revolution breaks out, they may merge with the vast millennial outburst: '*Rampok* bands sprang from the ground like mushrooms, speedily followed by roving groups of the populace, possessed with the expectation of a Mahdi or a millennium.' (This is a description of the Javanese movement after the defeat of the Japanese in 1945.)[6] Yet without the expected Messiah, charismatic leader, 'just king' (or whoever pretends to his crown), or – to continue our Indonesian illustration – the nationalist intellectuals headed by Sukarno who grafted themselves upon this movement, such phenomena are likely to subside, leaving behind them at best rearguard actions by backwoods guerrillas.

Still, when banditry and its companion, millennial exaltation, have reached such a peak of mobilization, the forces which turn revolt into a state-building or society-transforming movement do as often as not appear. In traditional societies accustomed to the rise and fall of political regimes which leave the basic social structure unaffected, gentry, noblemen, even officials and magistrates, may recognize the signs of impending change and consider the time ripe for a judicious transfer of loyalties to what will no doubt turn out to end with a new set of authorities, while expeditionary forces will think of changing sides. A new dynasty may arise, strong in the mandate of heaven, and peaceable men will settle down to their lives again, with hope, doubtless eventually with disillusion, reducing the bandits to the minimum of expected outlawry and sending the prophets back to their hedge-preaching. More rarely, a Messianic leader will appear to build a temporary New Jerusalem. In modern situations, revolutionary movements or organizations will take over. They too may well, after their triumph, find bandit activists drifting back into marginal outlawry, to join the last champions of the old way of life and other 'counter-revolutionaries' in increasingly hopeless resistance.

How indeed do social bandits come to terms with modern revolutionary movements, so remote from the ancient moral world in which they exist? The problem is comparatively easy in the case of national independence movements, since their aspirations can be readily expressed in terms comprehensible to archaic politics, however little they have in common with these in fact. This is why banditry fits into such movements with little trouble: Giuliano turned with equal ease into the hammer of the godless Communists and the champion of Sicilian separatism. Primitive movements of tribal or national resistance to conquest may develop the characteristic interplay of bandit guerrillas and populist or millennial sectarianism. In the Caucasus, where the resistance of the great Shamyl to the Russian conquest was based on the development of Muridism among the native Moslems, Muridism and other similar sects were said even in the early twentieth century to provide the celebrated bandit-patriot Zelim Khan (see p. 49 above) with aid, immunity and ideology. He always carried a portrait of Shamyl. In return, two new sects which sprang up among the Ingush mountaineers in that period, one of militants for holy war, the other of unarmed quietists, both equally ecstatic and possibly derived from the Bektashi, regarded Zelim Khan as a saint.[7]

It does not take much sophistication to recognize the conflict between 'our people' and 'foreigners', between the colonized and the colonizers. The peasants of the Hungarian plains who formed the bandit guerrillas of the famous Sandor Rózsa after the defeat of the revolution of 1848-9 may have been moved to rebellion by adventitious acts of the victorious Austrian regime, such as military conscription. (Reluctance to become or remain a soldier is a familiar source of outlaws.) But they were nevertheless 'national bandits', though their interpretation of nationalism might have been very different from the politicians'. The famous Manuel Garcia, 'King of the Cuban countryside', who was reputed single-handed to keep ten thousand soldiers occupied, naturally sent money to the father of Cuban independence, Martí, which the apostle refused, with the habitual dislike of most revolutionaries for criminals. Garcia was killed by treason in 1895, because – so Cuban opinion still holds – he was about to throw in his lot with the revolution.

National liberation bandits are therefore common enough, though commoner in situations where the national liberation movement can be derived from traditional social organization or resistance to foreigners than when it is a novel importation by schoolmasters and journalists. In the mountains of Greece, barely occupied, never effectively administered, the *klephtes* played a larger part in liberation than in Bulgaria, where the conversion to the national cause of eminent haiduks such as Panayot Hitov was notable news. (But then, the Greek mountains were allowed a fair measure of autonomy, through the formations of *armatoles*, technically policing them for the Turkish overlords, in practice doing so only when it suited them. Today's *armatole* captain might be tomorrow's klephtic chief, and the other way round.) What part they play in national liberation is another question.

It is harder for bandits to be integrated into modern movements of social and political revolution which are not primarily against foreigners. Not because they have any more difficulty in understanding, at least in principle, the slogans of liberty, equality and fraternity, of land and freedom, of democracy and communism, if expressed in language with which they are familiar. On the contrary, these are no more than evident truth, the marvel being that men can find the right words for it. 'Truth tickles everyone's nostrils,' says Surovkov, the savage Cossack, listening to Isaac Babel reading Lenin's speech from *Pravda*. 'The question is how it's to be pulled from the heap. But he goes and strikes at it straight off, like a hen pecking at a grain.' It is that these evident truths are associated with townsmen, educated men, gentry, with opposition to God and Tsar, i.e. with forces normally hostile or incomprehensible to backward peasants.

Still, the junction can be made. The great Pancho Villa was recruited by Madero's men in the Mexican Revolution, and became a formidable general of the revolutionary armies. Perhaps of all professional bandits in the Western world, he was the one with the most distinguished revolutionary career. When the emissaries of Madero visited him, he was readily convinced, especially as he was the only local bandit they wanted to recruit to the cause, though he had shown no previous interest in politics. Madero was a rich and educated man. If he was on the side of the people, this proved that he was selfless and the cause therefore untarnished. A man of the people himself, a man of honour, and whose standing in banditry was itself honoured by such an invitation, how could he hesitate to put his men and guns at the disposal of the revolution?[8]

Less eminent bandits may have joined the cause of revolution for very similar reasons. Not because they understood the complexities of democratic, socialist or even anarchist theory (though the last of these contains few complexities), but because the cause of the people and the poor was self-evidently just, and the revolutionaries demonstrated their trustworthiness by unselfishness, self-sacrifice and devotion – in other words, by *their personal behaviour*. That is why military service and jail, the places where bandits and modern revolutionaries are most likely to meet in conditions of equality and mutual trust, have seen many political conversions. The annals of modern Sardinian banditry contain several examples. That is also why the men who became the Bourbonist brigand leaders in 1861 were often the same men who had flocked to the standard of Garibaldi, who looked, spoke and acted like a 'true liberator of the people'.

Hence, where the ideological or personal junction between them and the militants of modern revolution can be made, the bandits may join the new-fangled movements as bandits or as individual peasants as they would have joined archaic ones. The Macedonian ones became the fighters of the Komitadji movement (the Internal Macedonian Revolutionary Organization or Imro) in the early twentieth century, and the village schoolmasters who organized them in turn copied the traditional pattern of haiduk guerrillas in their military structure. Just as the brigands of Bantam joined the Communist rising of 1926, the generality of Javanese followed the secular nationalism of Sukarno or the secular socialism of the Communist Party, the Chinese ones Mao Tse-tung, who was in turn powerfully influenced by the native tradition of popular resistance.

How could China be saved? The young Mao's answer was, 'Imitate the heroes of Liang Shan P'o', i.e. the free bandit guerrillas of the Water-Margin novel.[9] What is more, he systematically recruited them. Were they not fighters, and in their way socially conscious fighters? Did not the 'Red Beards', a formidable organization of horse-thieves which still flourished in Manchuria in the 1920s, forbid its members to attack women, old people and children, but obliged them to attack all civil servants and official personages, but 'if a man has a good reputation we shall leave him one half of his property; if he is corrupt we shall take all his possessions and baggage'? In 1929 the bulk of Mao's Red Army seems to have been composed of such 'declassed elements' (to use his own classification, 'soldiers, bandits, robbers, beggars and prostitutes'). Who was likely to run the risk of joining an outlaw formation in those days except outlaws? 'These people fight most courageously,' Mao had observed a few years earlier. 'When led in a just manner, they can become a revolutionary force.' Did they? They certainly gave the young Red Army something of the 'mentality of roving insurgents', though Mao hoped that 'intensified education' might remedy this.

We now know that the situation was more complicated than that.[10] Bandits and revolutionaries respected each other as outlaws with common enemies, and for much of the time roving Red Armies were not in a position to do more than what was expected of classic social bandits. However, both distrusted each other. Bandits were unreliable. The Communist Party continued to think of He Long, a bandit chief who became a general, and his men as 'bandits' who might defect at any moment, until he actually joined the Party. That may be partly because the lifestyle of a prosperous bandit chief hardly fitted in with the puritan expectations of the comrades. Still, while individual bandits and the occasional chief might be converted, unlike the revolutionaries, institutionalized banditry can work with the prevailing power structure as easily as it can reject it. 'Traditionally (Chinese banditry) formed the rudimentary stage in a process that could lead, under the right conditions, to the formation of a rebel movement whose objective was to gain the "Mandate of Heaven". In itself, though, it was not a rebellion and certainly not revolution.' Banditry and Communists met, but their ways diverged.

Undoubtedly political consciousness can do much to change the character of bandits. The communist peasant guerrillas of Colombia contain some fighters (but almost certainly not more than a modest minority) who have transferred to them from the former freebooting brigand guerrillas of the *Violencia*. 'Cuando bandoleaba' (When I was a bandit) is a phrase that may be heard in the conversations and reminiscences that fill so much of a guerrilla's time. The phrase itself indicates the awareness of the difference between a man's past and his present. However, probably Mao was too sanguine. Individual bandits may be easily integrated into political units, but collectively, in Colombia at least, they have proved rather unassimilable into left-wing guerrilla groups.

In any case as bandits their military potential was limited, their political potential even more so, as the brigand wars in southern Italy demonstrate. Their ideal unit was less than twenty men. Haiduk *voivodes* leading more than this were singled out in song and story, and in the Colombian *violencia* after 1948 the very large insurgent units were almost invariably communist rather than grass-roots rebels. Panayot Hitov reports that the *voivode* Ilio, faced with two to three hundred potential recruits, said this was far too many for a single band and they had better form several; he himself chose fifteen. Large forces were, as in Lampião's band, broken up into such sub-units, or temporary coalitions of separate formations. Tactically this made sense, but it indicated a basic incapacity of most grass-roots chiefs to equip and supply large units or to handle bodies of men beyond the direct control of a powerful personality. What is more, each chieftain jealously protected his sovereignty. Even Lampião's most loyal lieutenant, the 'blond devil' Corisco, though remaining sentimentally attached to his old chief, quarrelled with him and took his friends and followers away to form a separate band. The various emissaries and secret agents of the Bourbons who tried to introduce effective discipline and co-ordination into the brigand movement in the 1860s were as frustrated as all others who have attempted similar operations.

Politically, bandits were, as we have seen, incapable of

offering a real alternative to the peasants. Moreover, their traditionally ambiguous position between the men of power and the poor, as men of the people but contemptuous of the weak and the passive, as a force which in normal times operated within the existing social and political structure or on its margins, rather than against it, limited their revolutionary potential. They might dream of a free society of brothers, but the most obvious prospect of a successful bandit revolutionary was to become a landowner, like the gentry. Pancho Villa ended as a *hacendado*,* the natural reward of a Latin American aspirant *caudillo*,† though no doubt his background and manner made him more popular than the fine-skinned Creole aristocrats. And in any case, the heroic and undisciplined robber life did not fit a man much for either the hard, dun-coloured organization-world of the revolutionary fighters or the legality of post-revolutionary life. Few successful bandit insurgents seem to have played much of a role in Balkan countries they had helped to liberate. Often enough the heroic memories of freedom in the pre-revolutionary mountains, and national insurrection, merely lent an increasingly ironic glitter to strong-arm gangs in the new state, at the disposal of rival political bosses when they did not do a little freelance kidnapping and robbery for their private purposes. Nineteenth-century Greece, nourished on the klephtic mystique, became a gigantic spoils-system, whose prizes were thus competed for. The romantic poets, folklorists and philhellenes had given the highland brigands a European reputation. M. Edmond About, in the 1850s, was more struck by the shoddy reality of the 'Roi des Montagnes' than by the high-flown phrases of klephtic glory.

The bandits' contribution to modern revolutions was thus

---

* Large landowner, owner of estate (*hacienda*).
† Military chieftain establishing political power, a sadly familiar figure in Latin American history.

ambiguous, doubtful and short. That was their tragedy. As bandits they could at best, like Moses, discern the promised land. They could not reach it. The Algerian war of liberation began, characteristically enough, in the wild mountains of the Aurès, traditional brigand territory, but it was the very unbandit-like Army of National Liberation which finally won independence. The Chinese Red Army soon ceased to be a bandit-like formation. More than this. The Mexican Revolution contained two major peasant components: the typical bandit-based movement of Pancho Villa in the north, the mainly unbandit-like agrarian agitation of Zapata in Morelos. In military terms, Villa played an immeasurably more important part on the national scene, but neither the shape of Mexico nor even of Villa's own north-west was changed by it. Zapata's movement was entirely regional, its leader was killed in 1919, its military forces were of no great consequence. Yet this was the movement which injected the element of agrarian reform into the Mexican Revolution. The brigands produced a potential *caudillo* and a legend – not least, a legend of the only Mexican leader who tried to invade the land of the *gringos* in this century.[*] The peasant movement of Morelos produced a social revolution; one of the three which deserve the name in the history of Latin America.

---

[*] The most dramatic evidence of this comes from the village of San José de Gracia in the uplands of Michoacan, Mexico, which – like so many Mexican villages – expressed its popular aspirations by mobilizing under the banner of Christ the King *against* the revolution (as part of the *Cristero* movement, best known through Graham Greene's *The Power and the Glory*). Its excellent historian points out that it naturally 'abhorred the great figures of the Revolution' with two exceptions: President Cardenas (1934–40) for distributing the land and ending the persecution of religion, and Pancho Villa. 'These have become popular idols.'[11] Even in 1971 the general store in a very similar township of the same area, a place not visibly much given to literature, contained *The Memoirs of Pancho Villa*.

9

***

The Expropriators

Finally we must glance at what may be called 'quasi-banditry', that is to say at revolutionaries who do not themselves belong to the original world of Robin Hood, but who in one way or another adopt his methods and perhaps even his myth. The reasons for this may be partly ideological, as among the Bakuninist anarchists who idealized the bandit as

> the genuine and sole revolutionary – a revolutionary without fine phrases, without learned rhetoric, irreconcilable, indefatigable and indomitable, a popular and social revolutionary, non-political and independent of any estate (Bakunin).

They may be a reflection of the immaturity of revolutionaries who, though their ideologies are new, are steeped in the traditions of an ancient world, like the Andalusian anarchist guerrillas after the Civil War of 1936–9 who fell naturally into the ways of the old 'noble bandoleros', or the German journeymen of the early nineteenth century, who – equally naturally – called their secret revolutionary brotherhood, which eventually became Karl Marx's Communist League, the League of the Outlaws. (The Christian-communist tailor Weitling actually at one stage planned a revolutionary war waged by an army of outlaws.) Or else the reasons may be technical, as in guerrilla movements which are obliged to follow substantially similar tactics as social bandits, and on the cloak-and-dagger fringe of illegal revolutionary movements where the smugglers, terrorists, forgers, spies and 'expropriators' operate. In this chapter we shall deal primarily with 'expropriation', the long-established and tactful name for robberies designed to supply revolutionaries with funds. Some observations about contemporary phenomena of this kind will be found in the Postscript (see p. 189–99).

The history of this tactic remains to be written. Probably it appeared at the point where the libertarian and authoritarian lines of the modern revolutionary movement, the *sans-culottes* and the Jacobins, crossed: by Blanqui out of Bakunin. The place of birth was almost certainly the anarchist-cum-terrorist milieu of Tsarist Russia in the 1860s and 1870s. The bomb, which was the standard equipment of Russian expropriators in the early twentieth century, points to their terrorist derivation. (In the Western tradition of bank-robbery, whether political or ideologically neutral, the gun has always prevailed.) The term 'expropriation' itself was originally not so much a euphemism for hold-up jobs, as a reflection on a characteristically anarchist confusion between riot and revolt, between crime and revolution, which regarded not only the gangster as a truly libertarian insurrectionary, but such simple activities as looting as a step towards the spontaneous expropriation of the bourgeoisie by the oppressed. We need not blame serious anarchists for the excesses of the lunatic fringe of declassed intellectuals which indulged in such fancies. Even among them 'expropriation' gradually settled down as a technical term for robbing money for the good of the cause, normally – and significantly – from those symbols of the impersonal power of money, the banks.

Ironically enough, it was not so much the local and scattered forms of direct action by anarchists or *narodnik*[*] terrorists which made 'expropriation' a public scandal in the

[*] Member of the Russian populist revolutionary movements in the later nineteenth century.

international revolutionary movement, as the activities of the Bolsheviks during and after the 1905 revolution; and more particularly the famous Tiflis (Tbilisi) hold-up of 1907, which netted the party over 200,000 roubles, unfortunately mainly in large and readily traced denominations which got the devoted exiles like Litvinov (subsequently Commissar for Foreign Affairs of the USSR) and L. B. Krassin (subsequently in charge of Soviet foreign trade) into trouble with Western policemen, when they tried to change them. It was a good stick with which to beat Lenin, always suspect to other Russian sectors of social democracy for his alleged 'Blanquist' tendencies, just as later it was a good stick with which to beat Stalin, who, as a leading Bolshevik in Transcaucasia, was deeply involved in it. The accusations were unfair. Lenin's Bolsheviks differed from other social democrats merely in not condemning any form of revolutionary activity, including 'expropriations' *a priori*; or rather, in lacking the cant which officially condemned operations which, as we now know, not only illegal revolutionaries but also governments of all complexions practise whenever they think them essential. Lenin did his best to fence off 'expropriations' from ordinary crime and unorganized freebooting with an elaborate system of defences: they were to be conducted only under organized Party auspices, and in a framework of socialist ideology and education, in order not to degenerate into crime and 'prostitution'; they were to be undertaken only against state property, etc. Stalin, though no doubt he went into these activities with his usual lack of humanitarian scruple, was doing no more than applying party policy. Indeed, the 'expropriations' in turbulent and gun-happy Transcaucasia were neither the largest – the record was probably held by the Moscow hold-up of 1906, which netted 875,000 roubles – nor the most frequent. If anything Latvia, in which the Bolshevik papers publicly acknowledged at least some of the income from expropriations (as socialist journals usually record donations), was most given to this form of selfless robbery.

The study of the Bolshevik 'expropriations' is therefore not the best way to grasp the nature of such quasi-bandit activity. All that the hold-ups of official Marxists demonstrate is the obvious fact that such activities tend to attract a certain type of militant, the sort of man who, though often longing for the really high-status work such as drafting theoretical statements and addressing Congress, feels happier with a gun and a lot of presence of mind. The late 'Kamo' (Semeno Arzhakovich Ter-Petrossian, 1882–1922), a remarkably brave and tough Armenian terrorist who threw in his lot with the Bolsheviks, was a splendid example of such a political gun-fighter. He was the chief organizer of the Tiflis expropriation, though as a matter of principle never spending more than fifty copecks a day on his personal needs. The end of the civil war left him free to realize his long-cherished ambition to educate himself properly in Marxist theory, but after a brief interval he yearned once again for the excitements of direct action. He was probably lucky to die in a bicycle accident when he did. Neither his age nor the atmosphere of the Soviet Union in subsequent years would have been congenial to his type of Old Bolshevism.

The best way to bring the phenomenon of 'expropriation' before readers who have no great acquaintance with ideological gun-fighters, is to sketch the portrait of one of them. I choose the case of Francisco Sabaté Llopart (1913–60),[1] one of the group of anarchist guerrillas who raided Catalonia from bases in France after the Second World War, and almost all of whom are now dead or in jail: the Sabaté brothers, José Luis Facerias, the waiter from the Barrio Chino in Barcelona (probably the ablest and most intelligent), Ramon Capdevila, named 'Burntface' or 'Caraquemada', the boxer (probably the toughest, and one of the longest-lived – he lasted until 1963), Jaime Pares 'El Abissinio', the factory operative José Lopez Penedo, Julio Rodriguez 'El Cubano', Paco Martinez, Santiago Amir Gruana 'El Sheriff', Pedro Adrover Font 'El Yayo', the young and always hungry José Pedrez Pedrero 'Tragapanes', Victor Espallargas whose pacifist principles allowed him to take part in bank-raids but only unarmed, and all the others whose names now live only in police records and the memories of their families and a few anarchist militants.

Barcelona, that hill-compressed, hard-edged, and passionate capital of proletarian insurrection, was their *maquis*, though they knew enough about the mountains to make their way there and back. Commandeered taxis and stolen cars were their transport, bus-queues or the gates of football stadia their rendezvous. Their accoutrements were the raincoat so dear to urban gunmen from Dublin to the Mediterranean, and the shopping bag or briefcase to hide guns or bombs. 'The idea' of anarchism was their motive: that totally uncompromising and lunatic dream which a great many of us share, but which few except Spaniards have ever tried to act upon, at the cost of total defeat and impotence for their labour movement. Theirs was the world in which men are governed by pure morality as dictated by conscience; where there is no poverty, no government, no jails, no policemen, no compulsion and discipline except that of the inner light; no social bond except fraternity and love; no lies; no property; no bureaucracy. In this world men are pure like Sabaté, who never smoked or drank (except, of course, a little wine with meals) and ate like a shepherd even when he had just robbed a bank. In this world, reason and enlightenment bring men out of darkness. Nothing stands between us and this ideal except the forces of the devil, bourgeois, fascists, Stalinists, even backsliding anarchists, forces which must be swept away, though of course without our falling into the diabolical pitfalls of discipline and bureaucracy. It is a world in which the moralists are also gun-fighters, both because guns kill enemies and because they are the means of expression of men who cannot write the pamphlets or make the great speeches of which they dream. Propaganda by action replaces that by word.

Francisco Sabaté Llopart 'Quico' discovered 'the idea', in common with an entire generation of Barcelona working-class youths aged between thirteen and eighteen, in the great moral awakening which followed the proclamation of the Spanish Republic in 1931. He was one of five children of an unpolitical municipal watchman in Hospitalet de Llobregat, just outside Barcelona, and became a plumber. Except for Juan, a highly-strung boy who wanted to become a priest, the boys looked to the left, following Pepe the fitter, the eldest of the family. Francisco himself was not a great man for books, though later he was to make heroic efforts to read, in order to be able to discuss Rousseau, Herbert Spencer and Bakunin as a good anarchist should, and took even greater pride in his two daughters at the lycée in Toulouse, who merely read *Express* and *France-Observateur*. He was not semi-literate, and the Franco accusation that he was rankled bitterly.

He was seventeen when he joined the libertarian youth organization, and began to absorb the marvellous truth in the libertarian Athenaeums in which the young militants met for education and inspiration; for to be politically conscious in those days in Barcelona meant to become an anarchist as certainly as in Aberavon it meant to join the Labour Party. But no man can escape his fate. Sabaté was designed by nature for his subsequent career. Just as there are some women who are only fully themselves in bed, so there are men who only realize themselves in action. Big-jawed, thick-browed, looking smaller than his size because of his stockiness – though he was actually a little less muscular than he appeared – Sabaté was one of these. In repose he was nervous and awkward. He could barely sit in comfort in an armchair, let alone in a café in which, like a good gun-fighter, he automatically chose the seat with cover, a view of the door and in reach of the back exit. As soon as he stood with a gun on a street corner he became relaxed, and in a gruff way, radiant. 'Muy sereno', his comrades described him at such moments, sure of his reflexes and instincts, those hunches which can be perfected but not created by experience; sure above all of his courage and his luck. No man without remarkable natural aptitudes would have lasted nearly twenty-two years of unbroken outlawry, interrupted only by jail.

It seems that almost from the start he found himself in the *grupos específicos* or action groups of young libertarians, which fought duels with the police, assassinated reactionaries, rescued prisoners and expropriated banks for the purpose of financing some small journal, the distaste of anarchists for organization making regular fund-raising difficult. His activities were local. In 1936, by that time married – or rather demonstratively *not* married – to a servant-girl from Valencia, whose character had the same classic simplicity as his, he was still merely a member of the revolutionary committee in Hospitalet. He went to the front with the *Los Aguiluchos* (the 'Young Eagles') column, commanded by Garcia Oliver, as a centurion, responsible as the name implies, for a centuria of a hundred men. As his gifts for orthodox leadership were clearly small, he was soon sidetracked into an armourer's job, for which his familiarity with guns and explosives fitted him. Also, he had a natural bent for machinery, as for combat. He was the kind of man who builds himself a motor-bike from scrap. He never became an officer.

Sabaté fought quietly with his column (later merged into the 28th Ascaso Division, commanded by Gregorio Jover) until the battle of Teruel. He was not used for the special guerrilla units of the army, which suggests that his gifts were unrecognized. Then, during the battle, he deserted. The official explanation is that he quarrelled with the Communists, which is more than likely. He returned to lead a clandestine existence in Barcelona, and for practical purposes he never abandoned it for the rest of his life.

His first activity in Barcelona against the 'Stalino-bourgeois coalition' was to liberate a comrade wounded in a brush with the (Republican) police; his second, still under orders from the anarchist Youth Committee of Defence, to liberate four men imprisoned after the rising of May 1937, who were being transported between those two poles of the anarchist militant's globe, the Model Prison and the Fortress of Montjuich. Then he was himself imprisoned in Montjuich and tried to escape. His wife smuggled a gun to him in his next jail at Vich and he fought his way out. By now he was a marked man. His comrades therefore found a cover for him by sending him to the front with another anarchist unit, the 26th Durruti Division, with which he stayed to the end. It should perhaps be added for the benefit of non-anarchist readers that Sabaté's attachment to the Republican cause and hatred of Franco never wavered throughout these surprising proceedings.

The war ended. After the usual spell in a French concentration camp, Sabaté found himself working as a fitter near Angoulême. (His brother Pepe, an officer, had been caught and jailed in Valencia; young Manolo was barely twelve years old.) There the German occupation caught him, and soon pushed him back into clandestinity. But unlike many other Spanish refugees, his resistance activities were marginal. Spain, and only Spain was his passion. Around 1942 he was back on the Pyrenean border, ill but already anxious to raid. From this time he began to operate on his own, reconnoitring the frontier.

At first he went round the mountain farms as a travelling mechanic and general mender-of-things. Then, for a while, he joined a group of smugglers. Subsequently he established two bases for himself, settling as a small farmer in one of them, the Mas Casenobe Loubette near Coustouges, within sight of Spain. The frontier between La Preste and Ceret was to remain 'his' beat ever after. There he knew the routes and the people and had his bases and depots. This eventually doomed him, for it defined the area in which the police could expect him to be within a few kilometres. On the other hand it was inevitable. Efficient organizations can route couriers or guerrillas anywhere between Irun and Port Bou. A congeries of small craft enterprises, like the anarchist underground, is one of local men who are in darkness outside the small area they have themselves prospected. Sabaté knew his sector of the mountains. He knew the routes thence to Barcelona. Above all, he knew Barcelona. These were his 'manor'. There and nowhere else in Spain did he operate.

He seems not to have raided before the spring of 1945, though he did some guiding and perhaps liaison work. In May of that year he began to make a name for the rescue of a comrade from the police in the middle of Barcelona. And then came the events which made him a hero. One of his guerrilla parties attracted the attention of the Civil Guard in Bañolas, his dispersal point after crossing the mountains. The police flourished their arms – Sabaté was punctilious about not shooting until the other side made a move to draw – and one was killed, the other disarmed. He bypassed the hue-and-cry by the simple method of walking in easy stages to Barcelona. By the time he arrived the police was informed.

He walked straight into an ambush at the habitual meeting place of the comrades, a milk bar in the Calle Santa Teresa. Sabaté's hunch for ambushes was extraordinary. The four labourers coming slowly towards him chatting were, it was clear to him, policemen. He therefore continued slowly and carelessly walking *towards* them. At about thirty feet he reached for his sub-machine-gun and took aim.

The war between police and terrorists is one of nerves as well as of guns. Whoever is more frightened has lost the initiative. The key to Sabaté's unique career after 1945 lay in the moral superiority he established over the police by the conscious policy of always, when possible, advancing *towards* them. The four plain-clothes men were unnerved, made for cover, and opened a rather ragged fire while he got away. He did not shoot.

It was a sign of his relative inexperience that he now went home, to arrange for a meeting with his brother Pepe, who had just come out of prison in Valencia. The house was already watched, but Sabaté only went in for a moment to leave a note, and immediately left by the back to sleep in the woods. This seems to have taken the police by surprise. When he returned next morning he smelled the ambush, but it was too late. His route was already barred by a couple of obvious police wagons. He strolled carelessly past them. What he did not know was that one of the wagons contained two captured anarchists who were to identify him. They did not. Sabaté strolled casually on to safety.

The hero needs bravery for his role, and he had proved it. He needs guile and perspicacity. He needs luck, or in mythical terms, invulnerability. Surely, the man who smelled and escaped ambushes had proved these. But he also needs victory. He had not yet proved this – except by killing policemen – and by rational standards could never prove it. But by the standards of the poor, oppressed and ignorant men whose horizons are bounded by their *barrio** or at most their city, the mere capacity for the outlaw to survive against the concentrated forces of the rich and their jailers and police-men is victory enough. And henceforth nobody in Barce-lona, a city which breeds more competent judges of good rebels than most, could doubt that Sabaté possessed this capacity. Least of all himself.

The years 1944 to the early 1950s saw a systematic attempt to overthrow Franco by private invasions across the frontier from France, but more seriously, by guerrilla action. This episode is not widely known, though the attempts were serious enough. Official Communist sources list a total of 5,371 actions by guerrillas in the period between 1944 and 1949, with a peak of 1,317 in 1947, and Franco sources estimate guerrilla casualties of 400 in the largest *maquis*, in southern Aragon.[2] Though guerrillas operated in virtually all mountain areas, especially in the north and in southern Aragon, the Catalan guerrillas, who were almost wholly anarchist, unlike the others, were of no military significance. They were too poorly organized and undisciplined, and their objectives were those of their cadres, men with parish-pump perspectives. It was among such anarchist groups that Sabaté now operated.

Considerations of high politics, strategy and tactics, hardly affected men of his kind. For them such things were always shadowy unrealities, except insofar as they were vivid because symbolic of immorality. Theirs was an abstract world in which free men with guns stood on one side, policemen and jails on the other, typifying the human condition. Between them crouched the mass of undecided workers who would one day – perhaps tomorrow? – rise in majestic power, inspired by the example of morality and

* City quarter or district.

heroism. Sabaté and his friends found political rationalizations for their exploits. He put bombs into some Latin American consulates as a protest against a UN vote. He fired leaflets out of a home-made bazooka over the football crowds to make propaganda, and held up bars to play anti-Franco speeches on tape-recorders. He robbed banks for the cause. Yet those who knew him agree that what really counted for him was the example of action rather than its effect. What moved him, irresistibly and obsessively, was the desire to go raiding in Spain, and the eternal duel between the militants and the state: the plight of imprisoned comrades, the hatred of policemen. An outsider may wonder why none of the groups ever made a serious attempt to assassinate Franco or even the Captain-General of Catalonia, but only Signor Quintela of the Barcelona police. But Quintela was head of the 'Social Brigade'. He had, it was said, tortured comrades with his own hands. It is highly typical, not least of anarchist disorganization, that when Sabaté planned to assassinate him he found another group of activists already independently on the same trail.

From 1945 on, therefore, the heroic exploits and demonstrations multiplied. The official record (not altogether reliable) credits Sabaté with five attacks in 1947, one in 1948, and no less than fifteen in 1949, the year of the Barcelona guerrillas' glory and disaster. That January the Sabatés took charge of the job of raising funds for the defence of some prisoners, a list of whom a certain Ballester had brought out of jail together with a police tail. In February Pepe Sabaté shot a policeman who was ambushing the brothers at their rendezvous in the doorway of the Ciné Condal, by the Paralelo. Shortly after this the police surprised Pepe and José Lopez Penedo asleep in La Torrasa, a suburb of flamenco-singing southern immigrants, and they fought a gun-battle in their underwear between the front door and the dining-room. Lopez died; Pepe, badly wounded, escaped almost naked, swam the River Llobregat, held up a passer-by for clothes, and walked five miles to a safe refuge where he was joined by his brother, who got him a doctor and saw to his transport to France.

In March Sabaté and the Los Manos group of young Aragonese joined up to kill Quintela, but only killed a couple of lesser Falangists by mistake. (Someone had issued a general threat to attack the police headquarters, which frightened the police, but also warned them.) In May Sabaté and Facerias joined forces to put their bombs into the Brazilian, Peruvian and Bolivian consulates, Sabaté calmly dismantling one after the alarm had been given so as to exchange the time mechanism for immediate detonation. Other bombs he placed with the simple help of a fishing-rod. By the autumn, however, the police had the situation under control. In October Pepe fell in ambush, having just fought his way out of another over the dead body of a policeman. That month saw the end of the bulk of the fighting men.

In December a third of the Sabaté brothers went. Young Manolo had never been a man of 'the idea'. His ambition was to be a *torero*, and he had left home in his teens to follow the *novilladas** in Andalusia, but the adventure represented by his brothers was equally tempting. They did not let him join them, preferring him to study and better himself, but the Sabaté name got him into the group of the redoubtable Ramon Capdevila ('Caraquemada' or 'Burntface'), an ex-boxer who had abandoned the ring on getting 'the idea' and was now a considerable expert in explosives. One of the few guerrillas whose activities made some sense, he raided in the provinces, blowing up pylons and suchlike. Inexperienced, Manolo lost his way in the hills after a brush with the police,

---

* Bullfights for junior bulls and fighters.

and was arrested. The Sabaté name guaranteed his execution. He was shot in 1950, leaving behind nothing but a French watch.

By this time, however, Sabaté was no longer in Spain. Troubles, mainly with the French police, were to keep him away for nearly six years. They had begun in 1948 when he was stopped by a gendarme on one of his innumerable trips to the frontier in a hired car (Sabaté always liked transport which allowed him to keep his hands free). He had lost his head, broken and run. They had found his gun, and later a sizeable collection of equipment, explosives, radios, etc. in his farm at Coustouges. In November he was sentenced *in absentia* to three years in jail and a fine of 50,000 francs. On advice, he appealed and in June 1949 got a harmless two months, which was later raised to six, with five years' *interdiction de séjour*. Henceforth his visits to the frontier were to be illegal even from the French side, and he lived under police supervision far from the Pyrenees.

In fact, he did not get out of jail for a year, for the French police tied him to another and much more serious affair, a hold-up at the Rhône-Poulenc factory in May 1948, as a result of which a watchman had died. It is characteristic of the staggering unrealism of the activists, whose very existence depended on the benevolent blindness of the French authorities, that they expropriated the bourgeoisie for the good of the cause with as much readiness in Lyons as in Barcelona. (Only the intelligent Facerias avoided this; *he* robbed his non-Spanish banks in Italy.) It is equally typical that they left a back-trail as visible as a landing-strip. Thanks to some very good lawyers, the case against Sabaté was never quite proved; though the police had at one point lost patience and actually extracted a confession from him after beating him up for several days, or so his lawyer claimed, not without plausibility. After four *non-lieus* the case was still pending at the time of his death. However, in addition to considerable worry, the affair cost him the best part of another two years in jail.

When Sabaté got his head at least temporarily above these rough waters, he found the political situation utterly changed. In the early 1950s all parties abandoned guerrilla warfare for more realistic tactics. The militants were therefore alone.

It was a desperate blow. Sabaté, though quite incapable of obeying any instructions with which he disagreed, was a loyal man. Not to have the approval of the comrades hurt him almost physically, and until his death he made constant but unavailing efforts to regain it. The blow was not softened by an offer to settle him in Latin America. As well offer Othello a consular post in Paris instead of an army. And so, in April 1955 he was back in Barcelona. Early in 1956 he teamed up with Facerias for a joint operation – the two individualists soon split up – and stayed for several months, publishing a small journal, *El Combate*, and holding up the Banco Central two-handed with the aid of a dummy bomb. In November he was back again for a hold-up of the large textile firm Cubiertos y Tejados, which netted almost a million pesetas.

After that the French police, tipped off by the Spaniards, caught up with him again. He lost his base in La Preste, and was once again imprisoned. He got out of jail in May 1958, but was ill for the next few months after a bad operation for ulcers. Facerias had been killed meanwhile. Then he began to plan his next and last raid.

By this time he was alone, except for a few friends. Even the organization, by its silent disapproval, seemed to lend colour to the fascists and bourgeois who thought of him as a mere bandit. Even his friends told him, with complete accuracy, that another raid would be suicidal. He had aged notably. All he had left was his reputation as a hero and the passionate conviction which lent this otherwise not very articulate man a remarkable power to persuade. This he carried round the *émigré* meetings of France in defiance of police regulations, a stocky figure with a bulging briefcase who shied away from sitting in corners. He was *not* a bandit. The cause could *not* be left without champions in Spain. Who knows, perhaps he would be the Fidel Castro of his country? Could they not understand?

He got together a little money and talked a fair number of men, mostly inexperienced, into taking arms. He went with the first group, consisting of Antonio Miracle, a bank clerk relatively fresh from clandestinity, two youngsters of barely twenty, Rogelio Madrigal Torres and Martin Ruiz, and an otherwise unknown married man of thirty, a certain Conesa; all from Lyons and Clermont-Ferrand. The rest never made the journey. He saw his family again at the end of 1959, but without telling them his plans. And then he went to what all, except perhaps himself, knew to be his death.

It can at least be said that he died as he would have wished to. The group was picked up by the police within a few miles of the frontier, doubtless on a tip-off. They broke away. Two days later they were surrounded in a lonely farm and besieged for twelve hours. After the setting of the moon Sabaté stampeded the cattle with a hand-grenade and crept silently away after killing his last policeman; but wounded. All his companions were killed. Two days later, on 6 January, he held up the 6.20 train from Gerona to Barcelona at the small stop of Fornells and ordered the driver to go straight through. It was impossible; for at Massanet-Massanas all trains switch to electric traction. By this time Sabaté's foot-wound had turned septic. He limped, had a high fever, and kept himself going with morphine injections from his first-aid kit. The other two wounds, a graze behind the ear and an entry-and-exit wound in the shoulder, were less serious. He ate the engine-crew's breakfast.

At Massanet he slipped back into the post-van, climbed on the new electric engine and worked his way forward to the driver's cabin. He held up the new crew. They also told him that it was impossible, short of risking accidents, to drive straight to Barcelona in defiance of the timetable. At this stage I think he knew that he would die.

Shortly before the small town of San Celoni he made them slow down and jumped off. By this time the police had been alerted all along the line. He asked a carter for wine, for his fever made him thirsty, and drank it in great gulps. Then he asked an old woman for a doctor. She directed him to the other end of town. It seems he mistook the house of the doctor's servant – the surgery was empty – and knocked up a certain Francisco Berenguer, who was clearly suspicious of the haggard, unwashed figure in a boiler-suit with pistol and sub-machine-gun, and refused to let him in. They struggled. Two policemen appeared at the ends of the two streets at whose corner the two men wrestled. Sabaté bit Berenguer's hand to get at his pistol – he could no longer get at the Sten gun – and wounded one last policeman before he fell at the corner of the Calle San José and San Tecla.

'If he had not been wounded,' they say in San Celoni, 'they would not have got him; for the police were afraid.' But the best epitaph is that of one of his friends, a bricklayer in Perpignan, spoken before the Maillol Venus which graces that civilized town's centre. 'When we were young, and the Republic was founded, we were knightly though also spiritual (*caballeresco pero espiritual*). We have grown older, but not Sabaté. He was a *guerillero* by instinct. Yes, he was one of those Quixotes who come out of Spain.' It was said, and perhaps rightly, without irony.

But better than any formal epitaph, he received the final

accolade of the bandit hero, the champion of the oppressed, which is the refusal to believe in his death. 'They say', said a taxi-driver a few months after his end, 'that they fetched his father and sister to look at the body, and they looked at it and said: "It is not he, it is someone else".' 'They' were wrong in fact, but right in spirit, for he was the sort of man who deserved the legend. More: whose only possible reward could be heroic legend. By any rational and realistic standards his career was a waste of life. He never achieved anything, and indeed even the proceeds of his robberies were increasingly swallowed up by the spiralling costs of semi-private clandestinity – false papers, arms, bribes, etc. – so that little was left for propaganda. He never even looked like achieving anything except a death-sentence for anyone known to be associated with him. The theoretical justification of the insurrectionary, that the sheer will to make a revolution can catalyse the objective conditions for revolution, could not apply to him, since what he and his comrades did could not conceivably have produced a larger movement. Their own argument, simpler and more Homeric, that since men are good, brave and pure by nature, the mere sight of devotion and courage, repeated often enough, must shame them out of their torpor, had equally little chance of success. It could only produce legend.

By his purity and simplicity Sabaté was fitted to become a legend. He lived and died poor; until the end the wife of the celebrated bank-robber worked as a servant. He robbed banks not simply for money, but as a *torero* fights bulls, to demonstrate courage. Not for him the discovery of the astute Facerias, that the safest way of collecting money is to raid a certain kind of hotel at 2 a.m., certain that the solid bourgeois found there in bed with a variety of mistresses would give up his cash willingly and not talk to the police.* To take money

*Actually, Spanishness defeated even this plan; one wealthy lover, perhaps anxious to impress his youthful girlfriend, resisted and was killed.

without exposing oneself to risk, was unmanly – Sabaté always preferred to knock over a bank with fewer people than were technically required, for this reason – and conversely, to take money at the risk of one's own life was, in some moral sense, to *pay* for it. To walk always *towards* the police was not only a sound psychological tactic, but the hero's way. He could no doubt have forced the engine-crews of his train to drive through, though it might not have done him much good; but he could not, morally, risk the lives of men who did not fight him.

To become a public legend a man must have simple outlines. To be a tragic hero everything about him must be pared away, leaving him silhouetted against the horizon in the quintessential posture of his role, as Don Quixote is against his windmills, and the gun-fighters of the mythical West are, solitary in the white sunlight of their empty midday streets. That is how Francisco Sabaté Llopart stood. It is just that he should be so remembered, in the company of other heroes.

10

***

The Bandit as Symbol

We have so far looked at the reality of social bandits, and at their legend or myth chiefly as a source of information about that reality, or about the social roles bandits are supposed to play (and therefore often do), the values they are supposed to represent, their ideal — and therefore often also real — relationship with the people. Yet such legends operate not simply among those familiar with a particular bandit, or any bandits, but very much more widely and generally. The bandit is not only a man, but a symbol. In concluding this study of banditry, we must therefore also look at these remoter aspects of our subject. They are curious in at least two ways.

The bandit legend among the peasants themselves is peculiar, because the immense personal prestige of celebrated outlaws does not prevent their fame from being rather short-lived. As in so many other respects, Robin Hood, though in most ways the quintessence of bandit legend, is also rather untypical. No real original Robin Hood has ever been identified beyond dispute, whereas all other bandit heroes I have been able to check, however mythologized, can be traced back to some identifiable individual in some identifiable locality. If Robin Hood existed, he flourished before the fourteenth century, when the cycle is first recorded in writing. His legend has therefore been popular for a minimum of six hundred years. All other bandit heroes mentioned in this book (with the exception of the protagonists of the Chinese popular novels) are much more recent. Stenka Razin, the insurgent leader of the Russian poor, dates back to the 1670s, but the bulk of such figures whose legends were alive in the nineteenth century, when such ballads were systematically collected, only date back to the eighteenth – which therefore appears to be the golden age of bandit heroes: Janošik in Slovakia, Diego Corrientes in Andalusia, Mandrin in France, Rob Roy in Scotland, for that matter the criminals adapted into the social-bandit pantheon like Dick Turpin, Cartouche and Schinderhannes. Even in the Balkans, where the recorded history of haiduks and *klephtes* goes back to the fifteenth century, the earliest klephtic heroes who survive as such in the Greek ballads seem to be Christos Millionis (1740s) and Bukovallas, who flourished even later. It is inconceivable that men such as these should not have been the subjects of song and story earlier than this. Great brigand insurgents like Marco Sciarra of the late sixteenth century must have had their legend, and at least one of the great bandits of that extremely disturbed period – Serralonga in Catalonia – did become a popular hero whose memory survived into the nineteenth century; but this case may be unusual. Why are most of them forgotten?

It is possible that there were some changes in the popular culture of Western Europe which explain this efflorescence of bandit myths in the eighteenth century, but hard to account for what seems to be the similar chronology in Eastern Europe. One might suggest that the memory of a purely oral culture – and those who perpetuated the fame of bandit heroes were illiterate – is relatively short. Beyond a certain lapse of generations the memory of an individual merges with the collective picture of the legendary heroes of the past, the man with myth and ritual symbolism, so that a hero who happens to last beyond this span, like Robin Hood, can no longer be replaced in the context of real history. This is probably true, but not the whole truth. For oral memory can last longer than ten or twelve generations. Carlo Levi records that the peasants of the Basilicata in the 1930s remembered two episodes of history vividly though vaguely as 'their own': the time of the brigands seventy years ago, and the time of the great Hohenstaufen emperors seven centuries earlier. The sad truth is probably that the heroes of remote times survive because they are not *only* the heroes of the peasants. The great emperors had their clerks, chroniclers and poets, they left huge monuments of stone, they represent not the inhabitants of some lost corner of the highlands (which happens to be like so many other lost corners), but states, empires, entire peoples. So Skanderbeg and Marko Kraljevic survive from the Middle Ages in Albanian and Serbian epics, but Mihat the Herdsman and Juhasz Andras (Andras the Shepherd) against whom

> no gun has any power,
> the balls which the Pandurs aim against him
> he catches in his naked hand,[1]

disappear in time. The great bandit is stronger, more famous, his name lives longer than the ordinary peasant's, but he is no less mortal. He is immortal only because there will always be some other Mihat or Andras to take his gun into the hills or on to the wide plains.

The second peculiarity is more familiar.

Bandits belong to the peasantry. If the argument of this book is accepted, they cannot be understood except in the context of the sort of peasant society which, it is safe to guess, is as remote from most readers as ancient Egypt, and which is as surely doomed by history as the Stone Age. Yet the curious and astonishing fact about the bandit *myth* is that its appeal has always been far wider than its native environment. German literary historians have invented a special literary category, the *Räuberromantik* ('bandit romanticism') which has produced a large and by no means only Germanic supply of *Räuberromane* ('bandit novels'), none of them designed for reading by either peasants or bandits. The purely fictional bandit hero, a Rinaldo Rinaldini or Joaquin Murieta, is its characteristic by-product. But more remarkable still, the bandit hero survives the modern industrial revolution of culture, to appear, in his original form in television series about Robin Hood and his merry men, in a more modern version as the Western or gangster hero, in the mass media of the late-twentieth-century urban life.

That the official culture of countries in which social banditry is endemic, should reflect its importance, is natural. Cervantes put the celebrated Spanish robbers of the late sixteenth century into his works, as naturally as Walter Scott wrote about Rob Roy. Hungarian, Romanian, Czechoslovak and Turkish writers devote novels to real or imaginary bandit heroes, while – a slight twist – a modernizing Mexican novelist anxious to discredit the myth, attempts to cut the hero down to the size of ordinary criminals in *Los Bandidos del Rio Frio*.* In such countries both bandits and bandit myths are important facts of life, impossible to overlook.

The bandit myth is also comprehensible in highly urbanized countries which still possess a few empty spaces of 'outback' or 'west' to remind them of a sometimes imaginary heroic past, and to provide a concrete *locus* for nostalgia, a symbol of ancient and lost virtue, a spiritual Indian territory for which, like Huckleberry Finn, man can imagine himself 'lighting out' when the constraints of civilization become too

---

* I am thinking of Zsigmond Moricz's novel about Sandor Rósza, Panait Istrati's *Les Haidoucs*, Yashar Kemal's *Mehmed My Hawk*, and above all the remarkable *Der Räuber Nikola Schuhaj* of the Czech Ivan Olbracht.

much for him. There the outlaw and bushranger Ned Kelly still rides, as in the paintings of the Australian Sidney Nolan, a ghostly figure, tragic, menacing and fragile in his home-made armour, crossing and re-crossing the sun-bleached Australian hinterland, waiting for death.

Nevertheless there is more to the literary or popular cultural image of the bandit than the documentation of contemporary life in backward societies, the longing for lost innocence and adventure in advanced ones. There is what remains when we strip away the local and social framework of brigandage: a permanent emotion and a permanent role. There is freedom, heroism, and the dream of justice.

The myth of Robin Hood stresses the first and the third of these ideals. What survives from the medieval greenwood to appear on the television screen is the fellowship of free and equal men, the invulnerability to authority, and the championship of the weak, oppressed and cheated. The classical version of the bandit myth in high culture insists on the same elements. Schiller's robbers sing of the free life in the forest, while their chief, the noble Karl Moor, gives himself up that the reward for his capture can save a poor man. The Western and the gangster film insist on the second, the heroic element, even against the obstacle of conventional morality which confines heroism to the good, or at least the morally ambiguous gunman. Yet there is no denying it. The bandit is brave, both in action and as victim. He dies defiantly and well, and unnumbered boys from slums and suburbs, who possess nothing but the common but never-theless precious gift of strength and courage, can identify themselves with him. In a society in which men live by subservience, as ancillaries to machines of metal or moving parts of human machinery, the bandit lives and dies with a straight back. As we have seen, not every legendary bandit of history survives thus, to feed the dreams of urban frustration. In fact, hardly any of the great bandits of history survive the translation from agrarian to industrial society, except when they are virtually contemporary with it, or when they have already been embalmed in that resistant medium for time-travel, literature. Chapbooks about Lampião are printed today among the skyscrapers of São Paulo because every one of the millions of first-generation migrants from the Brazilian north-east knows about the great *cangaçeiro* who was killed in 1938, i.e. in the actual lifetimes of all who are more than sixty-two years old. Contrariwise, twentieth-century Englishmen and Americans know about Robin Hood 'who took from the rich and gave to the poor' and twentieth-century Chinese about 'the Opportune Rain Sung Chiang . . . who helps the needy and looks lightly upon silver', because writing and printing transformed a local and spoken tradition into a national and permanent form. One might say that the intellectuals have ensured the survival of the bandits.

In a sense, they still do so today. The rediscovery of the social bandits in our time is the work of intellectuals – of writers, of film-makers, even of historians. This book is part of the re-discovery. It has tried to explain the phenomenon of social banditry, but also to present heroes: Janošik, Sandor Rósza, Dovbuš, Doncho Vatach, Diego Corrientes, Jancu Jiano, Musolino, Giuliano, Bukovallas, Mihat the Herdsman, Andras the Shepherd, Santanon, Serralonga and Garcia, an endless battle-order of warriors, swift as stags, noble as falcons, cunning as foxes. Except for a few, nobody ever knew them thirty miles from their place of birth, but they were as important to their people as Napoleons or Bismarcks; almost certainly more important than the real Napoleon and Bismarck. Nobody who is insignificant has several hundred songs made about him, like Janošik. They are songs of pride, and of longing:

> The cuckoo has called
> On the dry branch
> They have killed Shuhaj
> And times are hard now.[2]

For the bandits belong to remembered history, as distinct from the official history of books. They are part of the history which is not so much a record of events and those who shaped them, as of the symbols of the theoretically controllable but actually uncontrolled factors which determine the world of the poor: of just kings and men who bring justice to the people. That is why the bandit legend still has power to move us. Let us leave the last word to Ivan Olbracht, who has written better about it than almost anyone else.

> Man has an insatiable longing for justice. In his soul he rebels against a social order which denies it to him, and whatever the world he lives in, he accuses either that social order or the entire material universe of injustice. Man is filled with a strange, stubborn urge to remember, to think things out and to change things; and in addition he carries within himself the wish to have what he cannot have – if only in the form of a fairy tale. That is perhaps the basis for the heroic sagas of all ages, all religions, all peoples and all classes.[3]

Including ours. That is why Robin Hood is our hero too, and will remain so.

Appendix A

* * *

Women and Banditry

Since bandits are notoriously given to womanizing, and both pride and status require such demonstrations of virility, the most usual role of women in banditry is as lovers. Anti-social bandits can supplement their sexual attractions by rape, which in certain circumstances can guarantee that the victims will not talk. ('They said they were doing all this to us so that we would be too ashamed to talk, and to show what they were capable of', a Colombian girl reported to the guerrillas she subsequently joined.)[1] However, as Machiavelli observed long ago, interfering with women is a certain way to become unpopular, and bandits who rely on popular support or connivance must keep their instincts in check. The rule in Lampião's band was never to rape ('except for good reasons', i.e. presumably for punishment, revenge and terror). Political peasant guerrillas apply this rule with the greatest rigour: 'We explain the rule: a guerrilla who rapes a woman, any woman, is court-martialled.' But, among both bandits and guerrillas, 'If it's a natural thing, if the woman agrees, then there's no problem.'[2]

Characteristically, women are visited by their bandit lovers, a fact which facilitates de facto polygyny. But cases of girls sharing the roving life of the men are not unknown, though bands which systematically allow this practice are probably rare. Lampião's seems to have been the only one in north-east Brazil. Even so, when the men went on a particularly long and dangerous expedition they preferred to leave the women behind, often against their will, since the presence of a man's girl would inhibit his casual amorous adventures 'out of respect for the regular companion'.[3]

The women in a band would not normally step outside their accepted sexual role. They carried no firearms, and normally took no part in the fighting. Maria Bonita, Lampião's wife, embroidered, sewed, cooked, sang, danced and had children in the middle of the bush . . . She was satisfied to follow her husband. When necessary she took part in the fighting, but in general she merely looked on, urging her husband not to take too many risks.[4] However, Dadá, the wife of his lieutenant Corisco, had more of the Lady Macbeth in her, and could well have commanded a band herself. There are obvious inconveniences in having what is virtually always a small minority of women in a band of men. Fear of a redoubtable chief can minimize them, or in groups with the high political consciousness of peasant guerrillas, the disciplined morality of the cause. This may be the main reason for the reluctance of bandits to take women with them, or to interfere with women prisoners. Nothing saps solidarity as much as sexual rivalry.

The second and less publicized role of women in banditry is as supporters and links with the outside world. Mostly, it is to be presumed, they help kinsmen, husbands or lovers. Not much needs to be said about this.

The third role is as bandits themselves. Few women are active fighters, but enough cases occur in the balladry of the Balkan haiduks (see Chapter 6)[5] to make us suspect that they are at least in certain parts of the world a recognized phenomenon. In the Peruvian department of Piura, for instance, several flourished during the period 1917–37, including some band-leaders; notably Rosa Palma from Chulucanas, who is said to have earned the respect even of the formidable Froilán Alama, the most famous chief of the time, the lesbian Rosa Ruirías from Morropón, a notably combative community, and Bárbara Ramos, sister of two bandits and companion of another, from the *hacienda* Huapalas.*[6] These girls were renowned as horsewomen, sharpshooters and for their bravery. Except for their sex, there seems to have been nothing to distinguish them from any other bandits. The history of Argentine brigandage contains one formidable *montonera* and highway robber, Martina Chapanay (1799–1860s), of Indian origin, who had fought alongside her man and continued to do so after his death.[8]

Although the great Chinese bandit novel *The Water Margin* contains heroic females, in China, as elsewhere, there were very few women rank-and-file bandits. Given the practice of foot-binding, which prevented women from walking freely, this is hardly surprising. (However, they were more common in regions of horseback banditry, and where feet were not bound, as among the Hakka minority.) More surprising is the significant number of women recorded as bandit chieftains from the Taipings on. (The formidable Su Sanniang, who enjoyed a powerful reputation for 'killing the rich and helping the poor' became the heroine of numerous poems.) Typically, they seem to have taken to banditry to avenge the death of their husbands, or, more rarely, other kin, which may explain why their own names are rarely recorded.

Revenge also moved the women bandits of Andalusia, where they are not only recorded (e.g. in the nineteenth-century Torralba of Lucena [who wore male dress] and Maria Márquez Zafra [La Marimacho]), but also occupy a special place in the bandit legend as *serranas* (mountain women).[9] The stereotypical *serrana* turns to outlawry in general and revenge on men in particular, because she has been 'dis-

---

* Nothing is known of their fate, and they are not recorded in the list of bandits arrested and killed in this area,[7] though this list contains some other women.

honoured', i.e. deflowered. Such an activist reaction to dishonour is no doubt relatively even rarer among women than among men, but champions of the more militant type of women's liberation may be gratified to note that even traditional societies recognize it. However, like so much about banditry, this subject awaits further research.

In so far as they are avenged, most 'dishonoured' women in the societies breeding banditry are likely to find champions in their menfolk. Defence of 'honour', i.e. largely the sexual 'honour' of women, is probably the most important single motive that has led men into outlawry in the classical bandit regions of the Mediterranean and the overseas Latin world. The bandit there combined the functions both of the Statue and of Don Juan; but in this, as in so many other respects, he shared the values of his social universe.

Appendix B

***

The Bandit Tradition

I

As every movie-goer and television-watcher knows, bandits, whatever their nature, tend to exist surrounded by clouds of myth and fiction. How do we discover the truth about them? How do we trace their myths?

Most of the bandits around whom such myths have formed are long dead: Robin Hood (if there was one) lived in the thirteenth century, though in Europe heroes based on figures from the sixteenth to eighteenth centuries are the most common, probably because the invention of printing made possible the main medium for the survival of ancient bandit memories, the cheap popular broadsheet or chap-book. Passing from one set of storytellers, from one place and public to another throughout the generations, such a mode of transmission can tell us very little of documentary value about the bandits themselves, except that, for whatever reason, their subjects are remembered. Unless they have left traces in the records of the law and the authorities who pursued them, we have hardly any direct contemporary evidence about them. Foreign travellers captured by bandits, notably in South-East Europe, have left such reports from the nineteenth century; journalists, anxious to interview more than willing young men in bandoleers, not before the twentieth. Nor can even their reports always be taken at face value, if only because outside witnesses rarely knew very

much about the local situation, even if they could understand, let alone speak the sometimes impenetrable local
patois, and resisted the demands of sensation-hungry news
editors. At the time this is being written, kidnapping
foreigners – for ransom or in order to bargain for concessions
from the government – has become fashionable in the
Arabian republic of Yemen. So far as I can judge, little
relevant information has been extracted from liberated
prisoners.

Tradition, of course, shapes our knowledge of even those
twentieth-century social bandits – and there are several –
about whom we have reliable first-hand knowledge. Both
they and those who reported their ventures are familiar from
childhood with the part of the 'good bandit' in the drama of
poor countrymen's lives, and cast themselves or him for
it. M. L. Guzman's *Memorias de Pancho Villa* are not only
based in part on Villa's own words, but are the work of a
man who was both a great Mexican literary figure and (in
the judgement of Villa's biographer) 'an extremely serious
scholar as well'.[1] Yet in Guzman's pages Villa's early career
conforms a good deal more to the Robin Hood stereotype
than it seems to have done in real life. This is even more so in
the case of the Sicilian bandit Giuliano, who lived and died in
the high noon of press photographers and celebrity interviews in exotic places. But he knew what was expected of
him ('How could a Giuliano, loving the poor and hating the
rich, ever turn against the masses of the workers?' he asked,
having just massacred several of them), and so did journalists
and novelists. Even his enemies, the Communists, correctly
predicting his end, regretted that it was 'unworthy of an
authentic son of the labouring people of Sicily', 'loved by the
people and surrounded by sympathy, admiration, respect and
fear'.[2] His contemporary reputation was such that, as an old
militant of the region told me, after the 1947 massacre at the

Portella della Ginestra nobody had supposed that it could possibly have been the work of Giuliano.

Convenient and old-established myths are also available for bandits such as avengers and haiduks whose reputation cannot dwell on social redistribution and sympathy for the poor, at least so long they are not simple agents of official law or government. (Many an otherwise hateful rural tough has acquired a public halo merely by being the enemy of army or police.) It is the stereotype of the warrior's honour, or, in Hollywood terms, of the cowboy hero. (Since, as we have seen, so many bandits came from specialized martial communities of pastoral raiders, whose military capacities were recognized by rulers, nothing was more familiar to their young men.) Honour and shame, as the anthropologists tell us, dominated the value-system in the Mediterranean, the classic region of Western bandit myth. Where available, feudal values reinforced it. Heroic robbers were, or regarded themselves as, 'noble', a status which – at least in theory – also implied moral standards worthy of respect and admiration. The association has survived into our distinctly non-aristocratic societies (as in 'gentlemanly behaviour' or 'a noble gesture' or *noblesse oblige*). 'Nobility' in this sense links the most brutal of the hard men with guns to the most idealized of Robin Hoods, who are indeed classified as 'noble robbers' ('edel Räuber') in several countries for this reason. The fact that a number of bandit chieftains celebrated in myth may actually have come from armigerous families (even if the term *Raubritter* – robber baron – does not appear in literature before the nineteenth-century liberal historians) strengthened the linkage.

Thus the first major entrance of the noble bandit into high culture (i.e. into the literature of the Golden Century of Spain) stresses both their supposed social status as gentlemen, i.e. their 'honour', as well as their generosity, not to mention (as in Lope de Vega's *Antonio Roca*, based on a Catalan brigand of the 1540s) the good sense of moderation in violence and not antagonizing the peasantry. The French memorialist Brantôme (1540–1614), echoing at least one contemporary judgement, described him in his *Vie des dames galantes* as 'one of the bravest, most valiant, shrewd, wary, capable and courteous bandits ever seen in Spain'. In Cervantes' *Don Quixote*, the bandit Rocaguinarda (active in the early seventeenth century) is even presented as specifically on the side of the weak and poor.[3] (Both were in fact of peasant origin.) The actual record of what has been called 'the Catalan Baroque bandits' is far from that of Robin Hoods. Does the ability of the great Spanish writers to produce a mythological version of noble banditry at the very time when the sixteenth- and seventeenth-century epidemic of real banditry was at its peak prove their remoteness from reality or simply the enormous social and psychological potential of the existence of the brigand as an ideal type? The question must be left open. In any case the suggestion that Cervantes, Lope, Tirso de Molina and the other glories of Castilian high culture are responsible for the later positive image of banditry in popular tradition, is implausible. Literature had no need to give robbers a potential social dimension.

The most perceptive history of the original Robin Hood's tradition has recognized this even among robbers who laid no claim to it.[4] It stresses 'the difficulty of defining crime, especially by the haziness of the borderline between crime and politics, and by the violence of political life' in fourteenth- and fifteenth-century England. 'Crime, local rivalries, the control of local government, the bringing to bear of the authority of the crown, all intermingled. This made it easier to imagine that the criminal had some right on his side. He gained social approval.' As in the value-system of Hollywood

Westerns, rough-and-ready justice, the violent redress of wrong (known as 'Folville's Law', after a knightly family famous for righting its own wrongs in this way) was a good thing. The poet William Langland (whose *Piers Plowman* – c. 1377 – incidentally contains the first reference to Robin Hood ballads) thought that Grace endowed men with the qualities to fight Antichrist, including

> Some to ride and recover what was wrongfully taken.
> He showed them how to regain it through the might of their
> hands
> And wrest it from false men by Folville's laws. (Prof. Holt's
> translation)

Contemporary public opinion, even outside the outlaw's own community, was therefore prepared to focus on socially commendable aspects of a celebrated bandit's activities, unless, of course, his reputation as an anti-social criminal was so shocking as to make him an enemy to all honest folk. (In that case tradition provided an alternative, which never-theless satisfied the public's appetite for highly-coloured drama in the form of no-holds-barred chapbook confessions by notorious malefactors which detailed their progress from an initial breach of the Ten Commandments through a horrifying criminal career, to a plea for divine and human forgiveness at the foot of the gallows.)

Naturally, the more remote the public was – in time or space – from a celebrated brigand, the easier it was to concentrate on his positive aspects, the easier to overlook the negative. Nevertheless the process of selective idealiza-tion can be traced back to the first generation. In societies with a bandit tradition, if, among other targets, a brigand attacked those of whom public opinion disapproved, he immediately acquired the entire Robin Hood legend – in-cluding impenetrable disguises, invulnerability, capture by treason and the rest (see Chapter 4). Thus Sergeant José Avalos, retired from the *gendarmerie* to farm in the Argentine Chaco, where he had himself in the 1930s pursued the celebrated bandit Maté Cosido (Segundo David Peralta, 1897–?), had no doubt at all that he had been a 'people's bandit'. He had never robbed good Argentines, but only the agents of the big international farm-produce corporations, 'los cobradores de la Bunge y de la Clayton'. ('Of course', as he put it to me when I interviewed the old frontiersman on his farm in the late 1960s, 'my trade [oficio] was to catch him, just as it was his trade [oficio] to be a bandit.)' I was therefore able to predict successfully what he would claim to remember about him.* It is indeed true that the famous bandit had held up the car of a representative of Bunge & Born, relieving him of 6,000 pesos in 1935; he had also held up a train which carried, among the other victims, presumably 'good Argentines', a man from Anderson, Clayton & Co. (12,000 pesos), and netted as much as 45,000 in a raid on a local office of Dreyfus – still, with Bunge, one of the biggest names in the global farm-produce trade – both in 1936. However, the record shows that the band's specialities, train-robbery and kidnapping for ransom, showed no patriotic discrimination.[5] It was the public that remembered the foreign exploiters and forgot the rest.

The situation was even clearer in feuding societies, where a 'legitimate' homicide was criminalized by the state; all the more so when hardly anybody believed in the impartiality of the state's justice. Giuseppe Musolino, a lone outlaw, from start to finish utterly refused to accept that he was a criminal in any sense, and indeed in jail refused to wear the criminal prisoner's uniform. He was neither bandit nor brigand, he had neither robbed nor stolen, but merely killed spies,

---

* I was reminded of this prediction in 1998 by Professor José Nun of Buenos Aires, with whom I had undertaken the trip to the Chaco.

informers and *infami*. Hence at least some of the extraordinary sympathy, almost veneration, and protection he enjoyed
in the countryside of his region of Calabria. He believed in
the old ways against the evil new ways. He was like the
people: living in bad times, unjustly treated, weak, victi-
mized. He was unlike them only in standing up against the
system. Who cared about the details of the local political
conflicts which had led to the original homicide?[6]

In a politically polarized situation, such selection was even
easier. Thus a classic Carpathian bandit legend has developed
in the Beskid Mountains of Poland around one Jan Salapatek
('The Eagle'), 1923–55, a resistance fighter in the Polish
Home Army during the war, who continued in the anti-
Communist resistance after the war, and who appears to have
remained an outlaw in the inaccessible highland forests until killed by the agents of the Cracow Security Service.[7]
Whatever the reality of his career, given the distrust of the
peasants for new regimes, his myth is indistinguishable from
the traditional legend of the good bandit – 'there are only
some superficial changes in it: an axe is replaced by an
automatic gun, a landlord's palace by communist cooperative
store and "starosta" by Stalinist Security Service'. The good
bandit wronged nobody. He stole from co-operatives but
never people. The good bandit always exists in contra-
distinction to the bad robber. So, unlike some, including
even some anti-Communist partisans, Salapatek wronged
nobody ('I remember there was partisan from the same
village – he was son of bitch' [*sic*]). He was the man who
helped poor people. He distributed sweets in the school yard,
went to the bank, brought money, 'threw it on the square
and said "take it, that's your money which does not belong to
the state"'. In proper legendary fashion, though oddly for a
guerrilla fighter against the regime, he used violence only in
self-defence and never initiated shooting. In short, 'he was

really just and wise, he was honestly fighting for Poland'. It may or may not be relevant that Salapatek was born in the same village as Pope John Paul II.

Indeed, since everyone in countries with a developed bandit tradition expected to see someone in the role of the noble bandit, including policemen, judges and brigands themselves, it was possible for a man to become a Robin Hood in his own lifetime, if he met the minimum requirements of the part. This was plainly the case with Jaime Alfonso 'El Barbudo' (1783–1824), as attested by reports in the *Correo Murciano* in 1821 and 1822 and in Lord Carnarvon's (1822) voyage through the Iberian Peninsula.[8] It was clearly also the case with Mamed Casanova, who flourished in Galicia in the early 1900s. He was described (and photographed) as 'el Musolino Gallego' by a Madrid journal (for Musolino, see also pp. 46, 55), as 'bandit and martyr' in the *Diario de Pontevedra*, and defended by a lawyer who subsequently became President of the Real Academia Gallega. He reminded the court in 1902 that ballads by folk-poets and romances sold on city streets attested to the popularity of his celebrated client.[9]

II

Some brigands can therefore acquire the legend of the good bandit in their own lifetime, or certainly in the lifetime of their contemporaries. Moreover, contrary to some sceptics, even famous bandits whose original reputation is unpolitical may soon acquire the useful attribute of being on the side of the poor. Robin Hood, whose social and political radicalism does not fully emerge until the 1795 collection of the Jacobin Joseph Ritson,[10] has social objectives even in the first, fifteenth-century version of his story: 'For he was a gode outlawe, And dyd pore men moch god.' Nevertheless, in its written form at least, in Europe the fully developed social bandit myth only appears in the nineteenth century, when even the least suitable candidates were apt to be idealized into champions of national or social struggle, or – under the inspiration of Romanticism – into men unconfined by the constraints of middle-class respectability. The vastly success-ful genre of German bandit novels of the early nineteenth century, has been summarized as: 'plots full of action . . . provided the middle-class reader with descriptions of vio-lence and sexual freedom . . . While crime has stereotypical roots in parental neglect, defective education and seduction by loose women, the ideal middle-class family, tidy, orderly, patriarchal and passions-reducing, is presented both as the ideal and the foundation of an ordered society.'[11] In China, of course, the myth is age-old: the first legendary bandits date back to the period of the 'warring states', 481–221 BC, and the great bandit classic, the sixteenth-century *Shuihu Zhuan*, based on a real band of the twelfth century, was as familiar to illiterate villagers from storytellers and itinerant drama troupes as it was to every educated young Chinese, not least Mao.[12]

Nineteenth-century Romanticism has certainly helped to shape the subsequent taste for the bandit as an image of national, social, or even personal liberation. I cannot deny that in some ways my view of 'haiduks' as 'a permanent and conscious focus of peasant insurrection' (see above, p. 78) was influenced by it. Nevertheless, the set of beliefs about social banditry is simply too strong and uniform to be reduced to an innovation of the nineteenth century or even a product of literary construction. Where the popular rural, and even city, public had a choice, it selected those parts of bandit literature or bandit reputation that fitted the social image. Roger Chartier's analysis of the literature on the bandit Guilleri (active in Poitou 1602–8) demonstrates that, given the choice between an essentially cruel gangster redeemed only by bravery and final contrition, and a man of good qualities who, though a bandit, was far less cruel and brutal than soldiers and princes, readers preferred the second. This was the basis of what from 1632 on became the first literary portrait in French of the classic and mythically stereotyped 'good bandit' ('le brigand au grand coeur'), qualified only by the requirement of state and church that criminals and sinners must not be allowed to get away with it.[13]

The process of selection is even clearer in a bandit without significant literary memorials, investigated both in the archives and by interviews with 135 aged informants in 1978–9.[14] The folk memory that survives about Nazzareno Guglielmi, 'Cinicchio', (1830–?) in the area of Umbria around his native Assisi, is the classic 'noble robber' myth. Although 'the figure of Cinicchio which emerges from archival research is not substantially in conflict with the oral tradition', in real life he was plainly not an ideal-typical Robin Hood. Yet while he made political alliances, and anticipated the later Mafioso methods by offering, for regular payments, to protect landowners against other bandits (not to mention himself), the oral tradition insists on his refusal to make deals with the rich and especially on his campaign of hatred and – significantly – *revenge* against Count Cesare Fiumi, who, it claims, had unjustly accused him. However, in this case there is also a more modern element in the myth. The bandit, who disappears from sight in the 1860s after organizing an escape to America, is supposed to have become very prosperous there, and at least one of his sons is said to have become a successful engineer. In late twentieth-century rural Italy, social mobility is also the reward of being a noble robber . . .

III

Which bandits are remembered? The number of those who survived the centuries in popular song and story is actually quite modest. Only about thirty songs about the banditry of sixteenth and seventeenth-century Catalonia were found by the folklore collectors of the nineteenth century and only about six of these are exclusively about particular bandits. (A third of the total are songs about the early seventeenth-century Unions *against* the attacks of bandits.) Not more than half-a-dozen Andalusian bandits became really famous. Only two Brazilian *cangaçeiro* chieftains – Antonio Silvino and Lampião – have made it into the national memory. Of nineteenth-century Valencian-Murcian bandits, only one acquired the myth.[15] Much, of course, may have been lost because of the impermanence of chapbooks and ballad sheets and the hostility of authorities, which sometimes penalized such material. Even more may never have reached print, or escaped the explorations of the earlier folklorists. A work published in 1947 mentions two examples of the religious cults around the graves of some dead brigands in Argentina (see p. 55 above); a later inquiry discovered at least eight. With one exception, none had attracted the attention of the educated public.[16]

Nevertheless, there is clearly some process that selects some bands and their leaders for national, or even international, fame while leaving others to local antiquarians or obscurity. Whatever it is that initially singles them out, the medium of their fame until the twentieth century was print. Since all the films about famous bandits known to me are based on figures first established by ballad, chapbook and newspaper reports, it may even be argued that this is still the case today, in spite of the retreat of the printed word (outside the computer screen) before the moving image of film, television and video. However, the memory of *bandits* has also been preserved by their association with particular places, such as Robin Hood's Sherwood Forest and Nottingham (locations dismissed by historical research), the Mount Liang of the Chinese bandit epic (in Shandong province) and several anonymous 'robber's caves' on Welsh, and doubtless other, mountainsides. The special case of shrines devoted to the cults of dead bandits has been considered above.

Yet tracing the traditions by which particular bandits have been chosen for fame and survival is less interesting than tracing the changes in the collective tradition of banditry. Here there is a considerable difference between the places where banditry, if it ever occurred on any significant scale, is beyond living memory, and those where it is not. This is what distinguishes Britain, or the last three centuries in the Midi of France ('where we have no record of large bands'[17]) from countries like Chechnya, where it is very much alive today, and those in Latin America, where it is within the memory of men and women who are still alive. Somewhere between these are the countries where the memory of nineteenth-century banditry or its equivalent is kept alive, partly by national tradition but mostly by the modern mass media, so that it can still act as a model of personal style, like the Wild West in the USA, or even of political action, like the Argentine guerrillas of the 1970s who saw themselves as the successors of the *montoneros* whose name they adopted, a choice which, their historian holds, enormously increased their appeal to potential recruits and the public.[18] In countries of the first kind, the memory of real bandits is dead, or has been overlaid by other models of social protest. What survives is assimilated to the standard bandit myth. This has already been discussed at length.

Much the most interesting are the countries of the second

kind. So it may be useful to conclude this chapter with some reflections on three of them, where the very different itinerary of the national bandit tradition can be compared: Mexico, Brazil and Colombia.[19] All three are countries which became familiar with large-scale banditry in the course of their history.

All travellers along its roads agreed that, if any Latin American state was quintessentially bandit country, it was nineteenth-century Mexico. Moreover, in the first sixty years of independence the breakdown of government and economy, war and civil war gave any body of armed men which lived by the gun considerable leverage, or at least the choice between joining army or police force on government pay (which, then as later, did not exclude extortion) or sticking to simple brigandage. Benito Juarez's Liberals, in their civil wars, lacking more traditional patronage, used them extensively. However, the bandits around whom the popular myths formed were those of the stable era of Porfirio Diaz's dictatorship (1884–1911) which preceded the Mexican Revolution. These bandits could be seen, even at the time, as challengers of authority and the established order. Later, with sympathetic hindsight, they might appear as precursors of the Mexican Revolution.[20] Thanks chiefly to Pancho Villa, the most eminent of all brigands turned revolutionaries, this has brought banditry a unique degree of national legitimacy in Mexico, though not in the USA, where in those very years violent, cruel and greedy Mexican bandits became the standard villains of Hollywood, at least until 1922 when the Mexican government threatened to ban all films made by offending movie companies from the country.[21] Of the other bandits who became nationally famous in their lifetime – Jesus Arriaga (Chucho El Roto) in central Mexico, Heraclio Bernal in Sinaloa, and Santana

Rodriguez Palafox (Santanon) in Veracruz – at least the first two still enjoy popularity. Bernal, killed in 1889, who was in and out of politics, is probably the most famous in the age of the media, celebrated in thirteen songs, four poems, and four movies, some adapted for television, but I suspect that the impudent Catholic but anti-clerical trickster Chucho (died 1885), who has also made it on to the TV screens, remains closer to the heart of the people.

Unlike Mexico, Brazil moved from colony to independent empire without disruption. It was the First Republic (1889–1930) which produced, at least in the grim hinterlands of the north-east, the social and political conditions for epidemic banditry: that is to say, transformed the groups of armed retainers tied to particular territories and elite families into independent operators roaming over the area of perhaps 100,000 square kilometres covering four or five states. The great *cangaçeiros* of the period 1890–1940 soon became regionally famous, their reputation spread orally and in chapbooks, which appear in Brazil not earlier than 1900,[22] by local poets and singers. Mass migration to the cities of the south and growing literacy were later to spread this literature to the shops and market stalls of the monster cities like São Paulo. The modern media brought the *cangaçeiros*, an obvious local equivalent to the Wild West, on to cinema and television screens, all the more readily as the most famous of them, Lampião, was actually the first great bandit to be filmed live in the field.* Of the two most celebrated bandits, Silvino acquired a 'noble robber' myth in his lifetime, which was reinforced by journalists and others to contrast with the great but hardly benevolent reputation of Lampião, his successor as the 'king of the backlands'.

Yet it is the political and intellectual co-option of the

---

* When Pancho Villa was filmed by the Mutual Film Corporation in 1914 it was as the revolutionary general.

cangaçeiros into Brazilian national tradition that is interesting. They were very soon romanticized by north-eastern writers, and, in any case, were easy to turn into demonstrations of the corruption and injustice of political authority. Insofar as Lampião was a potential factor in national politics, they attracted wider attention. The Communist International even thought of him as a possible revolutionary guerrilla leader, perhaps suggested by the leader of the Brazilian Communist Party, Luis Carlos Prestes, who in his earlier career as leader of the 'Long March' of military rebels came into contact with Lampião (see pp. 100–101). However, the bandits do not seem to have played a major part in the important attempt by the Brazilian intellectuals of the 1930s to build a concept of Brazil with popular and social as against elite and political bricks. It was in the 1960s and 1970s that a new generation of intellectuals transformed the *cangaçeiro* into a symbol of Brazilianness, of the fight for freedom and the power of the oppressed; in short, as 'a national symbol of resistance and even revolution'.[23] This in turn affects the way he is presented in the mass media, even though the popular chapbook/oral tradition was still alive among north-easterners, at least in the 1970s.

The Colombian tradition has followed a very different trajectory. It is, for obvious reasons, completely overshadowed by the bloodthirsty experience of the era after 1948 (or, as some historians prefer, 1946) known as *La Violencia* and its aftermath. This was essentially a conflict combining class warfare, regionalism and political partisanship of rural populations identifying themselves, as in the republics of the River Plate, with one or other of the country's traditional parties, in this case the Liberals and Conservatives, which turned into guerrilla war in several regions after 1948, and eventually (apart from the regions where the now powerful Communist guerrilla movement developed in the 1960s) into a congeries of defeated, formerly political armed bands, relying on local alliances with men of power and peasant sympathy, both of which they eventually lost. They were wiped out in the 1960s. The memory they have left has been well described by the best experts on the subject:

> Perhaps, except for the idealized memory that the peasants still hold in their old zones of support, the 'social bandit' has also been defeated as a mythical character . . . What took place in Colombia was the opposite process from that of the Brazilian *cangaço*. Over time the *cangaço* lost much of its characteristic ambiguity and developed towards the image of the ideal social bandit. The *cangaçeiro* ended up as a national symbol of native virtues and the embodiment of national independence . . . In Colombia, on the contrary, the bandit personifies a cruel and inhuman monster or, in the best of cases, the 'son of the *Violencia*', frustrated, disoriented and manipulated by local leaders. This has been the image accepted by public opinion.[24]

Whatever the images of the FARC (Fuerzas Armadas de la Revolución Colombiana – the chief guerrilla force in Colombia since 1964) guerrillas, paramilitaries and drug-cartel gunmen that will survive into the twenty-first century, they will no longer have anything in common with the old bandit myth.

What, finally, of the oldest and most permanent tradition of social banditry, that of China? Egalitarian or at least at odds with the strictly hierarchical ideal of Confucius, representing a certain moral ideal (carrying out 'the Way on Heaven's behalf'), it survived two millennia. What of the bandit rebels like Bai Lang (1873–1915) about whom they sang:

> Bai Lang, Bai Lang –
> He robs the rich to aid the poor,

And carries out the Way on Heaven's behalf.
Everyone agrees that Bai Lang's fine:
In two years rich and poor will all be levelled.[25]

It is hard to imagine that the decades of the warlord and bandit pandemic that followed the end of the Chinese Empire in 1911 will be remembered with much affection by anyone who experienced them. Nevertheless, though the scope for banditry declined dramatically after 1949, one would suspect that the bandit tradition survived well enough in the traditional 'bandit regions' of the still essentially rural China of the first decades of communism, in spite of Party hostility. We may suppose that it will migrate into the new giant cities which suck in poor country people in their millions in China as in Brazil. Moreover the great literary monuments to the bandit life, like the *Shuihu Zhuan*, will certainly continue as part of educated Chinese culture. Perhaps they will find a future, both popular and highbrow, on twenty-first-century Chinese screens, like that discovered for the not entirely dissimilar samurai roving sword-fighters and knights errant on those of twentieth-century Japan. One suspects that their potential as romantic myths is far from exhausted.

Postscript

* * *

This postscript to the text consists of two parts. The first considers the main criticisms of my original thesis on banditry for the benefit of readers who are interested in academic arguments. The second reflects on the survival of the classic model of social banditry in the age of developed capitalist economies up to the present.

I

A number of lines of criticism have been developed against the original 'social banditry' thesis.

The first and most fundamental was formulated by Anton Blok in the early 1970s[1] and widely taken up since. Blok did not deny that 'social banditry' in my sense exists, for 'in the initial phase of their career, outlaws and bandits embodied peasant resentment. By ransoming the rich, stealing their cattle, and sacking their *masserie*, bandits became folk heroes for doing what most of their fellows would have liked to do.' However unless they lacked protection, they did not last long, and peasants, lacking power, were, almost by definition, the weakest source of protection. So the outlaw who begins by redressing some personal wrong would 'either (be) killed or drawn into and constrained by the power domains of the established regional elites' and 'thus represented the other side of the class war'. Not to mention the fact that there were plenty of plain, socially unaffiliated robbers and thieves.[2] None of this conflicts with the argument of my book, although Blok's view that 'we should treat brigandage and bandit myth as forces that weaken peasant mobilization' needs modification.

Nevertheless, Blok's observation that 'what is wrong with Hobsbawm's perception of brigandage is that it pays too much attention to the peasants and the bandits themselves', i.e. not enough to the larger society and its structures of power and politics, is well taken. These matters were by no means neglected in my book (e.g. in Chapter 7), and a wider framework of historical analysis is lightly sketched. As I have myself observed, however, 'a model concentrating on the, real or ascribed, social protest function of the bandit may not be the most suitable framework for . . . analysis . . . since this must consider the totality of the phenomenon, whether classifiable as social protest or not. Thus the crucial question about the wave of Mediterranean banditry in the late sixteenth century is not whether Sciarra can be properly considered a social bandit.'[3] Of course my book was and is concerned primarily with 'the social protest function of the bandit'. However, the chapter on the relation of banditry to politics which I have added to this edition may help to make it a more balanced introduction to the subject. Banditry, it is clear, cannot be understood outside the context of politics.

On the other hand, for Blok the 'myth' of Robin Hood social banditry, which undoubtedly embodies a social aspiration of peasants, deserves historical study, but has very little to do with social reality. To put the matter simply – perhaps too simply – Robin Hood exists only in the minds of his public. But if there were no relation between bandit reality and bandit myth, any robber chieftain could become a Robin Hood. However, while the most unsuitable candidates have indeed sometimes been cast for the role, so far as I know, *all* regions with established bandit myths distinguish between 'good' bandits and primarily anti-social 'bad' bandits on the grounds of their behaviour in real life (actual or supposed). In the Chaco, Maté Cosido was considered a 'good' robber even by the police who pursued him and a certain Velázquez a bad one. The brothers Mesazgi (see pp. 1–5) were of uncertain status by the criteria of local opinion, since people disagreed about whether the feud which drove them into outlawry was really legitimate. However, once their actions helped the people, they were seen as 'special bandits'.

The only clear case of social banditry in eighteenth-century Germany was that of Mathias Klostermayer and his band in Bavaria ('der bayrische Hiesel'), who flourished around 1770. Since he specialized in poaching, an activity peasants always regarded as legitimate, he was admired and helped. 'Many hundreds', he claimed, 'have told me: come to my fields, there's too much game, you can see a hundred head or more.' He waged his private war against hunters, gamekeepers, law officers and other officials undisguised and in public, and had the reputation of never robbing anyone except these, his 'enemies'. When he attacked and sacked the public office (Amtshaus) in Täfertingen near Augsburg in broad daylight, he saw his raid as 'a lawful act' and evidently the peasants shared his view.[4] And by no means every Argentine gaucho bandit received the ultimate public accolade of sanctity. They had to be martyrs. The minimum condition was that 'he fought against official justice and especially against the institution of the police, and fell in this battle'. The woman bandit Martina Chapanay, otherwise much idealized, did not receive such popular canonization because 'she never fell victim to authority'.[5] Of course this might confirm realistic observers like Giuseppe Giarizzo, the eminent Sicilian historian of that island which discourages romantic illusions, in the belief I once heard him express, that the bandit myth is essentially a combination of consolation and falsification.

Conversely, given the universality and standard character of the bandit myth, would it be surprising if the outlaw who finds himself, for whatever reason, cast for this prestigious part in the scenario of rural life, tried at least sometimes, other things being equal, to act according to the script? No doubt dead bandits, or even remote ones, are more easily turned into Robin Hoods, whatever their actual behaviour. Yet there is some evidence that some bandits have, at least sometimes, tried to live up to their role. In the late 1960s the functionaries of the Communist Party in Bihar, India (CPI), tried vainly to dissuade a peasant activist who had graduated from freelance attacks on landlords to communist militancy, from distributing the money he collected for the Party directly to the peasants. He had always distributed money: it was hard to get out of the habit.

A second line of criticism seeks to undermine the class character of both banditry and even the bandit myth, by linking both to the world of the local ruling class rather than the peasantry. Thus both analysts of the original Robin Hood cycle and of the twentieth-century Brazilian *cangaçeiro* ballads point to their notable lack of interest in the specific concerns of their supposed constituency, the contemporary peasantry.[6] It is also evident that the homicides which cast so many young men into outlawry are highly likely to arise out of local family and political feuds, that is to say the rivalries of locally influential families. But the thesis of *Bandits*, which is not unaware of gentleman-robbers and local political rivalries, was not that virtually all brigandage should be seen as a manifestation of peasant protest (this is correctly described by Blok as 'the widespread vulgarization of Hobsbawm's model of social banditry') and still less that robbers are of interest only to peasants. Indeed, one of the major components of the bandit myth, the heroic and preferably selfless knight-errant righter of wrongs, the sword-fighter (as in Kurosawa's Samurai epics) or gunfighter (as in the Westerns) does not belong specifically to peasant societies. It appealed to spirited young men of all classes and notably to those of the arms-bearing ones. (How far it did so to young women must be left an open question.) And yet, whatever the nature of the original public for this or that ballad cycle, the essence of the bandit myth is social redistribution and justice for the poor. And most of the poor were peasants, as were the great majority of those who became bandits.

A third and more specific line of criticism takes aim at the types of bandit I describe as 'haiduks', that is to say bandit groups in permanent existence as potential 'primitive movements of guerrilla resistance and liberation'. This view, I now accept, was influenced by the image of the haiduk as fighter for freedom and national liberation, which has been described as a 'topos of the romantic era'. Nevertheless, the subsequent significance of the 'haiduk model' for Balkan revolutionaries has also been underlined.[7] Furthermore, experts on the Ottoman Empire and the Balkans, notably Fikret Adanir, have argued convincingly that one cannot simply talk of 'peasants' in an area where the balance between settled agriculture and nomadic or transhumant pastoralism was for centuries fluctuating and unstable. All the more so since haiduks seem to have come chiefly from the specialized communities of herdsmen.[8]

Nevertheless, the 'military strata sprung from the free peasantry' (pastoral or otherwise) remain both an example of freedom and potential resistance to authority and an example to other peasants not so fortunately situated – and also to later ideologists – even when they were, like so many communities on some empire's military frontiers, attached to and therefore integrated into, the imperial system. (The biographer of the most famous bandit revolutionary has recently reminded us of a Western equivalent, the free peasant 'military colonists' against the Apaches on the frontier of the Spanish empire in Mexico.[9]) Like the Argentine *gauchos* who saw themselves as enemies of state and legal authority even as they served lords and aspirants to the presidency, the Greek warrior lineages who resisted the Ottoman authority or served it, saw themselves as independent of it. And 'what collective memory has retained is conflict: the klephtic songs are about a clear division between the world of primitive rebellion . . . and the legal world represented by the Ottoman authorities and the notables. Whatever adjustments were made to produce a modus vivendi between the two, the division existed and could not be effaced.'[10]

However, my original thesis that social bandits, unlike the 'underworld' and communities of raiders by vocation, remain part of the peasant moral universe may be more undermined than I thought by the fact, which I had noted incidentally, that permanently existing and structured bandit formations constitute separate and self-regarding social communities. Like the anti-society of the criminal underworld, they developed special forms of behaviour and languages (argots) to distinguish themselves from the rest, although the 'Selected List of Bandit Slang' in Billingsley's *Bandits in Republican China* does not suggest that the specific vocabulary of Chinese bandits went much beyond expressions for specific bandit activities and euphemism. Yet they remained committed to the moral foundations of community and their empire, unlike such bodies as Anton Blok's deliberately blasphemous *Bokkerijders*, consciously representing the opposition to Christian society.

This brings me to the fourth line of criticism, the opposite of the first three, which argues that the distinction between social and other kinds of banditry is wrong because *all* crime is in some sense social protest and rebellion. The major expression of this view is Carsten Küther's study of the eighteenth-century German criminal underworld, which criticizes my book accordingly.[11] Elements of the same argument may be discovered in Blok's major study of one such gang, the formidable Dutch *Bokkerijders* (1730–74).[12]

This argument requires a little more space, not only because the problem of the 'underworld' is only glanced at in the main text, but because it raises important questions about the structure of European societies, particularly the profound, and now largely forgotten, distinction between 'honourable' ('ehrlich') or 'respectable' and 'dishonourable' ('unehrlich') or unrespectable occupations which ran right through them.[13] Social bandits never ceased to be part of society in the eyes of the peasants, whatever the authorities said, whereas the criminal underworld formed an outgroup and was largely recruited from outgroups. The very fact that in German the words 'ehrlich' and 'unehrlich', though derived from the word for 'honour' have acquired the primary meaning of 'honest' and 'dishonest', is significant. As usual, the disinction is less clear in practice than in theory. Social bandits, like the rest of the settled peasantry, belonged to the 'straight' world of respectable or 'honourable' ('ehrlich') people, whereas criminals, who often used to and still sometimes describe themselves as 'bent' or 'crooked' ('krumm'), do not. For the underworld, the distinction was equally clear: in Germany they were the smart 'Kochemer' (the term, like so much in German criminal argot was derived from Hebrew or rather Yiddish); the others were the stupid and ignorant 'Wittische'. However, people can readily be recruited from the first into the second, even though a large part of the pre-industrial underworld consisted of members of traditional outcast groups or hereditary criminal family networks. Thus in May 1819 a local band of criminals in Swabia (West Germany) posted notices in the fields with the following text:

> If you don't mind the gallows
> And you don't like to work
> Come and join me:
> I need stout fellows!
>
> Captain of a gang of 250 rogues.*

And indeed, as might be expected, the gangs contained some people described as the children of 'honest' parents.

The question at issue is the nature of this underworld or fringe world. It consisted essentially of two overlapping components: minorities of outcasts or 'strangers' living among the settled 'honest' folk and the footloose and vagrant. One might perhaps add the handful of 'unrespectable' individuals and families which existed in every village – the equivalents of Huck Finn's father, or for that matter Huckleberry Finn himself. To a large extent they were functionally integrated into 'straight' or 'respectable' society, though they did not form part of it: Jews were needed to trade cattle, knackers followed a necessary if despised trade, knife-grinders, tinkers, travelling hawkers were indispensable, not to mention the fairground folk who formed the pre-industrial entertainment industry. Since European society did not formally recognize castes, the separateness and the frequently hereditary character of such outgroups is easily recognizable only in ethnically definable cases such as the Jews and the gypsies. Nevertheless, unofficially they formed

---

* Anon., *Der schwarze Veri und die letzten Räuberbanden Oberschwabens* (Wangen im Allgäu, 1977), p. 9. The book, to which Mrs Alice Eisler has drawn my attention, appears to be a reprint of a volume in the library of the Princes zu Waldburg-Wolfegg. The gang or gangs concerned were nowhere near 250 strong.

something like a stratum of outsiders and outcasts. Curiously enough, they were sometimes employed by the authorities because of their very position outside the community: the executioner is a good example. In Bavaria, court bailiffs, process servers, and similar minor agents of government were frequently recruited from among these outcast ('unehrliche') professions: hence, it has been suggested (by Küther), the particularly marked hostility with which they were treated by the Bavarian Hiesel, who, as a social bandit, represented the 'honest' world of the peasantry.

To some extent these groups were not functionally integrated at any given moment; especially during the many times of famine, war, or otherwise generated crisis and social disorder, when the roads of Europe were filled with uprooted men and women, begging, stealing, and looking for work. There is no doubt that this vagrant population could be enormously large. For Germany it has been estimated at perhaps 10 per cent of the total population in the eighteenth century: a mass of men – and in bad times of women – composed of the travelling professions, those looking for work or, like journeymen artisans, passing through their institutionalized years of wandering, of 'sturdy beggars' (45 per cent of French vagrant delinquents reached a height which only 10.5 per cent of the general population attained[14]), of what the French called 'gens sans aveu' – vagabonds without even a notional place in the social order.

The view that the criminal classes were social protesters rests on the argument that they were linked to this large, oppressed and discriminated underclass, settled or vagrant, in ways analogous to those which linked the social bandit to peasant society, and 'represented' their interests. It has even been argued that criminal bandits were *more* socially revolutionary than Robin Hoods, since they represented a challenge to the existence of authority and the state itself, whereas, as we have seen, social bandits in themselves did not.

There is indeed no doubt that the rogue bands found aid and support among the outcast population and the socially marginal. There is also no doubt that almost any member of this population might, and if vagrant probably would, be drawn at some time into the sort of actions which not only the authorities but also the settled local population would regard as criminal. In times when vagrancy rose steeply, 'in spite of frequent demonstrations of solidarity with and acts of compassion for true misery, the image of "God's pauper" gave way to the image of the dangerous stranger, the person who had chosen the road that leads to crime'.[15] It was not only the rising bourgeois, with his puritan ethic, but the common labouring people of the countryside, less well protected than the townsmen, who called for draconian measures against the idle, vagrant and foreign poor. Thirdly, there is no doubt that the rogue bands relied systematically and deliberately, and could not have operated without, a network of support, shelter, and supply mainly among the outsiders of the countryside.

Yet social and criminal bandits are not comparable, even though in the eyes of the official law they were equally delinquent, because in the eyes of the common people's morality the one were criminal and the other were not. The distinction between acts which are not regarded as anti-social and acts which are may be drawn very differently according to time, place, and social environment, but it exists in all societies. Mitigating circumstances for acts agreed to be anti-social or 'immoral' may usually be recognized in certain cases, and among the poor and weak or those who can sympathize with them they may be more generously recognized: but that does not change the anti-social character of such acts.* Some societies are more tolerant than others. Nevertheless, all recognize the distinction between what is 'criminal' (immoral) and what is not. Confusion arises in the minds of observers who apply the criteria of other times and places, or those of other social groups (including the 'authorities'); and students who try to establish an analogy between social and criminal banditry sometimes fall into such confusion.

Let us consider a society – or sub-society – which was very loosely structured, highly individualist – indeed virtually acephalous in its rejection of internal and external authority – and unusually tolerant. 'I don't reckon we was what you mought call narrer-minded,' recalled an old Arkie from the Ozarks in the 1930s, '– not 'bout most things anyhow . . . We never done nothin' hasty, but if a feller . . . kept on stealin', he'd find a letter on his door some mornin' sayin' how folks was gettin' sick and tired o' sich goin's on and advisin' him t'git plumb out o'th' district afore the moon changed. Some called us bald-knobbers, some called us white-cappers, an' some called us night-riders, but 'mongst th' home folks we was jest th' committee.'[16] Hillbillies had their own definition of crime – but they had one. On the other hand the 'epidemic of bank-robbery' which swept the old Indian territory in the hard times after 1914 was different. Not only bandits but ordinary citizens robbed banks. The bankers of eastern Oklahoma could not rely on insurance guards (many insurance companies cancelled policies because 'public sentiment against banks was so severe as to encourage robberies') or local law officers, some of whom actually sympathized with the robbers. In fact 'there is no doubt of a most dangerous sentiment among a large element of the

---

* In the 'jurisprudence' of peasant societies, in which people know one another as families and individuals, there is usually no sharp line between judging the acts and the 'character' of the persons who commit them.

people that there is little crime in robbing a bank'.[17] Bank-robbery might be theoretically punishable by law, like distilling moonshine or (for most citizens in the 1980s) smuggling goods through customs or illegal parking, but it was not a real crime. It might in fact be an approved act of social justice.

As always, the distinction between the one kind of action and the other, or between those who carry them out, is often hazy in practice; especially when the actions are the same. This is why hoodlums can be admired, or even acquire the reputation of justicers if they rob unpopular institutions, or are believed to, and do not obviously victimize common folk. Even today train-robbers are not often regarded as enemies of the people, though in recent years there have been few cases like Al Jennings, the terror of the railroads in Indian territory, who ran a strong populist campaign for the Democratic gubernatorial nomination in Oklahoma in 1914, showing a film depicting his exploits as an outlaw throughout the state to full houses.[18] An anti-social hillbilly, expelled from his Ozark community, might well turn up elsewhere as an outlaw hero. Moreover, there was no sharp line, especially in hard times, and on the margin of settled society, between the regular folks and the outcasts, the vagrants, the outsiders. Revolutionaries who worked among them might, like the Wobblies, succeed in 'moralizing' many hobo jungle camps by banning drink and drugs in them, but it is a fair guess that the freight trains were ridden by many who would prey on anyone they could, rich or poor, even if, for the sake of safe travelling, they took out the red card when they had to. Even if, as is not unlikely, they sympathized vaguely with the struggle against injustice. It may be that in the settled rural world of pre-industrial society the line between 'regular' and 'irregular' people was more sharply drawn, if only because the distinction between members of the community and 'strangers' was much clearer, as also within the community the status of individuals and families. Below a certain level of status and livelihood, there was inevitably some overlapping, but the difference remained, and people, including the outsiders, were conscious of it.

So, whatever elements of social dissidence we detect in social banditry and the criminal underworld, Macheath and Robin Hood are not really comparable, and neither are their supporters. They operated differently: Robin Hood could call on the goodwill of every man who was not a personal enemy or an agent of authority; for highwaymen, the countryside was not so much a sea in which they swam, but rather – at best – a desert through which they rode, relying on a few known oases and places of shelter, their network of thieves' inns and fences.* Social bandits were a special form of countrymen, distinguished from the rest only by the ability to straighten their backs and above all by the willingness to do so. They lived aboveground – and they continued to do so even if they exchanged the role of peasant bandits for that of the lords' or the state's retainers. Rogues lived in their underworld: an underworld far more distinct from 'straight' society than our urban and business civilization can conceive. Social bandits could be, and were, people of whom their society could be proud. Rogues were heroes only among the marginal and the outcast, unless they acquired the reputation of social bandits, in which case the myth turned them into non-criminals. Even traditional communities of outsiders, insofar as they were communities, hesitated to acknowledge them publicly. Even today Jews, willing to claim revolutionaries who reject their Jewishness as their own – a Marx or a Trotsky – are apologetic about their Meyer Lanskys.

---

* Even these often claimed to offer their services only under duress, as may well have been the case in lonely and isolated taverns and homesteads.

Whether the criminal outsider was more of a social rebel than the peasant bandit is a question which need not detain us here. Neither in himself was much of a revolutionary by modern standards, as this book has tried to show for the social bandits. Perhaps in revolutionary times both might find themselves fighting in the ranks of the revolution, though the evidence that the rogues did so out of conviction in the great revolutions of modern Europe is extremely thin. China may have been different. The point to note is that in the times when both flourished, revolutions could be made by appealing to the constituency of the social bandits but not to that of the criminal rebels. This was not merely because settled peasant society contained a great many more people than the marginal rural underclass, fixed or vagrant, but because it was a society: old or new, just or unjust. Insofar as it excluded or marginalized the outsiders, it did not change its character. Insofar as they excluded themselves from it, they still defined themselves by their relation to it and depended for their operations on it. If the two lived in symbiosis, as they largely did, it was an unequal symbiosis. 'Straight' society could function without more than marginal reliance on the outcasts. They could not function at all except in the interstices of 'straight' society.

Hence the 'straight' society of the peasants including the peasant bandits functioned in terms of 'law' – God's law and the common custom, which was different from the state's or the lords' law, but nevertheless a social order. And insofar as it conceived of a better society it thought of it as the return to an old law or even, at moments, the advance to a new law which might bring not only true justice but freedom. The outcasts, except to some extent those who were members of permanent structured communities such as gypsies and Jews, had only the option of rejecting the law – God's, the people's as well as the lords' and the king's. That is what made them potential or actual criminals. They had no alternative vision of society and no implicit, let alone explicit, programme, only a justified resentment against the social order which cast them out, and alienation from it, a knowledge of injustice. Therein lay their tragedy.

There are no doubt good reasons why some recent students of banditry have tried to assimilate the criminal bandit to the social bandit, though (like Küther) well aware of the distinctions between them and their frequent mutual hostility. The similarity of the *modus operandi* of rogue bands with that of some recent political raiders and terrorists has not passed unperceived. They also operated in conditions of clandestinity, rarely mobilized except for specific operations, between which they disappear into the anonymity of urban middle-class society as the rogues melted into that of the marginal population. They also rely on a nationwide or even international network of support and contact, small in numbers but impressively wide and mobile. It may be that the neo-anarchist mood of some of the post-1960s ultra-left has encouraged the belief that crime as such is a form of revolutionary activity, as Bakunin had already suggested. Moreover, modern revolutionaries of the fringe, disillusioned with the mass of the 'regular' working population, which is now apparently integrated into the consumer society, and also apt to seek for the true and irreconcilable enemies of the status quo among marginal groups and outsiders, may well now look on the marginals of the past, the 'unrespectable' underclasses, with more sympathy than did the old-fashioned peasant rebels or organized proletarian militants. And indeed, by any impartial standards, their condition was particularly oppressed and pitiful, their treatment by the 'honest' world was indefensible. The emancipation of humanity cannot be confined to respectable people alone. The unrespectable also rebel in their fashion. The point of my argument is not to disagree with those who analyse the history of pre-industrial crime as a sort of social protest. It is simply to point out that what there is of social rebellion in the Macheath of *The Threepenny Opera* is not the same as that in Robin Hood. Nor are the two comparable.

The fifth and most convincing criticism of my book is the one I have already accepted in the Preface to this edition. It concerns my uncritical use of the literature and legend of banditry as a source. Very little about the historical reality of social banditry, let alone the career of any actual bandit, can be inferred from the content of the myths told about them or the songs sung about them. And insofar as anything can be inferred, it can only be after a close and critical study of their textual history, such as was entirely absent from the original version of my argument. Of course this does not affect such texts as sources for what people believed about, or wanted from, or read into, banditry, although even here more caution is needed than I sometimes showed.

At least one much more specific criticism on Sardinian banditry should also be mentioned, though it applies more to the general line of Sardinian studies than to my occasional references in earlier editions of *Bandits*.[19] It has been noted that the specific identification of Sardinian banditry with the pastoral Barbagia highlands, which was assumed to be an area of particularly archaic social structure, only came into existence in the late nineteenth century. This, it is argued plausibly, is a consequence of the rise of a specialized and virtually exclusive cheese-export economy in sheep products in these highlands, but not elsewhere. It has since taken the form of systematic cattle-rustling, increasingly merging (since the 1960s) with kidnapping or ransom. I am not in a position to judge how far David Moss's specific explanation of this phenomenon in terms of the relations between the differently structured highland and semi-highland villages ('an activity which mediates opposed values yet keeps them distinct') has been accepted by others with Sardinian expertise.

Finally, I have been rightly criticized by writers stimulated by my model of 'social banditry' for confining it to premodern agrarian societies. Very similar phenomena occurred in nineteenth-century Australia and the nineteenth- and twentieth-century USA, which clearly belong neither to 'traditional peasantry' nor are they pre-capitalist or pre-industrial societies. As one student of the subject (L. Glenn Seretan) observes: 'social banditry is more polymorphous and resilient than Hobsbawm supposed and . . . the vagaries of American (or any other EJH) historical evolution were quite capable of casting up authentic variants' – even as late as F. D. Roosevelt's New Deal years. On the other hand I cannot accept the argument of my main 'modernist' critic, Pat O'Malley – an expert on Ned Kelly and the Australian bushrangers, who regards the social banditry in traditional peasantries as a special case of a more general situation likely to generate social banditry, namely a) 'the presence of chronic class struggle which is reflected in a unified conflict consciousness among direct producers' and b) 'the absence of institutional political organization of the interests of the producers which manifests a programme of effective action for the generalized attainment of their commonly sought ends'. True, condition b) occurs mainly in the pre-industrial era, but it can also be found later. For the same reason O'Malley is sceptical of my suggestion that the decline of social banditry has much to do with the improvement of modern transport, communication and rural law enforcement. He thinks social banditry can flourish in spite of them. However, his own subsequent work argues that English highwaymen disappeared in the early nineteenth century when faced with better policing organization and methods, but he ascribes this to 'their lack of a unified social class basis'.[20]

Actually, there is not much to argue about. Of course banditry as a social phenomenon diminishes when better ways of agrarian struggle become available. I have said so for forty years. It is equally plausible that its attraction is not exhausted even in an obviously capitalist society such as the USA, provided that it is a society in which the legend of social banditry is part of popular culture. This was the case in the USA of the 1930s. 'The premier outlaws of the 1930s', writes Seretan, 'were well aware that they belonged to a tradition: they were weaned on it and influenced by it; they paid obeisance to it in word and deed; and the trajectory of their brief spectacular careers was ultimately defined by it.' In the minds of such as Alvin Karpis, Bonnie Parker and Clyde Barrow, Robin Hood and Jesse James were alive and well and moving across the plains in automobiles.

None of this changes the fact that in a fully capitalist society the conditions in which social banditry on the old model can persist or revive are exceptional. They will remain exceptional, even when there is far more scope for brigandage than for centuries, in a millennium that begins with the weakening or even the disintegration of modern state power, and the general availability of portable, but highly lethal, means of destruction to unofficial groups of armed men. In fact, to no one's surprise, in most 'developed countries' – even in their most traditionalist rural areas – Robin Hood is by now extinct, for practical purposes. The analysis of my book was more concerned to explain the end of this age-old and widespread phenomenon than to define the possible conditions for its occasional revival and survival.

However, something needs to be said about the survival

and modification of social banditry in plainly capitalist rural societies.

II

The transition to a capitalist agriculture is complicated and lengthy, and since much of this agriculture continues to be conducted by family farmers who are really, technology apart, not all that different from the old-style peasants from whom many of them are descended, there is plenty of overlap – certainly culturally – between the old and the new rural worlds. Even when these new worlds are found beyond the ocean. Farming, after all, remains an industry of small enterprise compared to the scale of operations of industry and finance, not least in terms of workers employed per firm. Moreover, the ancient hostility of country to city, of countrymen to outsiders, visibly persists in the form of conflicts between the interests of farmers as a business group and the rest, as witness the problem of the European Economic Community. In the countryside the advance of the capitalist economy therefore provided some scope – for how long is a matter of argument – for a certain 'modernization' of social banditry.

It created novel targets for popular discontents (including that of capitalist farmers) and consequently new 'enemies of the people' against whom bandits could champion the people. Brazilian and US rural society did not share the city enthusiasm for railroads, partly because it wanted to keep out government and strangers, partly because it regarded railroad companies as exploiters. Brazilian *cangaçeiros* opposed railroad construction, and Governor Crittenden of Missouri hailed the killing of Jesse James as 'the relief of the state from a great hindrance to its prosperity and as likely to give an important stimulus to real estate speculation, to railroad enterprise and foreign immigration'.

However, much the most obvious of the new plagues which beset agriculturalists were banks and mortgages. As we have seen, Australian 'selectors', Argentinian and US frontier farmers were acutely conscious of these. Ned Kelly's bushrangers did not practise highway robbery at all, but concentrated on bank-raids. The James brothers notoriously specialized in banks and railroads. As we have also seen, there was probably no redneck in the South-west and few prairie farmers anywhere in times of depression who would not have regarded this as natural and just. The chief reason why Maté Cosido did not rob Argentine banks, an equally natural target, was that local farmers recognized an even more devilish agent of impersonal capital than native finance, namely foreign finance. While the admirers of Janošik and Musolino knew about debt, it is only in an essentially capitalist economy that bank credits, mortgages and the like become central features of what farmers or peasants see as their exploitation and, incidentally, features which link the discontent of country people to that of other classes such as artisans and small traders. To this extent the period which turns institutions like banks into quintessential public villains and bank-robbery into the most readily understood form of robbing the rich marks the adaptation of social banditry to capitalism.

It could only be a partial and temporary adaptation, even though it is clear that the favourable image of the country or small-town boy (and, with Bonnie and Clyde, girl) as a sort of social bandit survived in the USA deep into the Depression of the 1930s. It has been shown to colour the image of figures like Dillinger and Pretty Boy Floyd, which perhaps one powerful reason why these rather minor and marginal figures on the scene of American crime were singled out as 'public enemies'. Unlike 'the mob', they represented a challenge to the all-American values of free enterprise, though they believed in it. Yet, as has been pointed out in the case of the James brothers, by the time they flourished, Grangerism and Populism were a more coherent response to the problems facing the rural Midwest than robbery. As politics, it was by now anachronistic.* The 'social' scope for banditry was contracting, and, while the Jameses continued to enjoy the ancient reputation of Robin Hoods, which their popular reputation and to some extent their career reproduce, a closer look at them shows them to be a variety of rural entrepreneurs – though 'keeping most of the habits and prejudices of their class intact'. They certainly did not belong to the poor, but (like most of the Confederate guerrillas of Jackson County, Missouri, who gave birth to the James gang) were the elder sons of well-to-do slave-holding farmers fighting against loss of property and status.[21]

The impact of a modern capitalist economy on a far more traditional type of banditry, that of the Sardinian highlands, has been dramatized recently by the evident transformation of shepherd-bandits into systematic kidnappers extorting enormous ransom payments. Kidnapping had until the 1960s been rather sporadic, and for revenge as often as for ransom. The new kidnapping wave was the direct conse-quence of the sudden and massive economic development of that decade in the Sardinian lowlands and coastlands; in some way it can be seen as part of the resistance of a traditional society against modernization, of lean and poor highlanders, bypassed by the great boom, against the new fat cats, local and foreign, of the coast. And certainly it kept some of the characteristics of the ancient shepherd banditry, harsh but

---

*My assessment of the James boys owes a great deal to a most valuable paper by Richard White, 'Western Outlaws and Social Bandits', which I have freely pillaged.

with its own ethical rules.* But it is clear that the new technique was now increasingly a means (if not for the actual shepherd-kidnappers then for the *prinzipales* and other highland entrepreneurs who instigated and employed them) to acquire large capital sums quickly in order themselves to invest in the now valuable coastal real estate: banditry merged into Mafia,[22] social protest disappeared behind criminal enterprise.

So, in its final historical stages – and few people really believe that Robin Hood is not on the way to permanent extinction – the role of the rural social bandit is transformed, insofar as it is played on a new stage, that of a modern capitalist/industrial society, amid new social, economic and technological scenery, and possibly by new actors, who can no longer be adequately described as traditional peasants, representatives of an old society struggling against the new, or champions of the rural poor. Little by little the rural bandit may even gently disentangle himself from the countryside and transfer to the city. The James gang after 1873 visited their home base in western Missouri only occasionally and discovered, as Frank James pointed out, that safety lay in anonymity rather than support from rural admirers. The Jameses did not let themselves be photographed, few men knew them by sight even in Clay and Jackson counties, and they relied largely on kinsfolk rather than the community at large for support, though probably traditional bandits also preferred blood relatives. But anonymity was easier in the city, and that is where the Jameses appear to have gravitated. For it is the city which is the place of secrets, the country where, at least for its inhabitants, everything is immediately known. There are times, even today, when countrymen's

---

* Cf. the treatment by their captors of a British mother and daughter kidnapped in 1979–80 and the local sense of outrage, which contributed to the liberation of the women, at the bandits' breach of a duly negotiated settlement.

knowledge is collectively withheld from outsiders, as in North Wales, where a consensus of silence protects those who burn the second homes of Englishmen against police inquiries. But perhaps today such rural *omertà* (as the Sicilians would call it) rests on forms of ideology, such as modern nationalism, on which traditional social bandits were not yet, or only incidentally, able to call.

The bandit myth also survives in the modern urbanized world as a sort of folk memory injected with new life periodically by the public media and the private resentment of the weak. Everyone has personal experience of being unjustly treated by individuals and institutions, and the poor, weak and helpless have it a lot of the time. And insofar as the myth of the bandit represents not only freedom, heroism and the dream of a general justice, but more especially personal insurgence against personal injustice, the righting of *my* individual wrongs, the idea of the individual justicer survives, particularly among those who lack the collective organizations which are the main line of defence against such wrongs. There are plenty of people on the underside of modern urban society who feel this. Perhaps, as the state becomes more remote and such bodies as unions contract into sectional self-defence organizations (as happens in some countries), the appeal of such dreams of private insurgence and private justice will grow. I doubt whether in our societies bandit-figures are the main ways of giving imagined expression to it. Jesse James and even John Wayne can no longer compete with Batman and his like. Survivals of the classical bandit dream in the big city need not therefore detain us long.

However, in the 1960s and 1970s a curious postscript to the history of traditional social banditry developed when its strategies and in some ways its ethos and ideals were transferred to a new social constituency, essentially of small bodies of middle-class youth who formed the core of neo-revolutionary groups, found a mass resonance from time to time on the enormously swollen university campuses of these decades, and attempted to bypass the old working classes and labour movements (of whatever political colour) by appealing directly to the unorganized poor and especially the alienated marginal and underclasses of society. Similarities with the Russian *narodnik* intellectuals have been suggested. A good deal of the new youthful cultural and political dissidence has been described as a kind of 'primitive rebellion', notably by the French sociologist Alain Touraine. Some of it may actually have considered itself in this light.[*] And some examples of such neo-primitivism (swathed in the ideological costume of the period) come to mind.

The 'Symbionese Liberation Army' (1973–4), an otherwise negligible episode on the wilder fringes of Californian alienation, may be compared with old-style private insurgency just because it insisted so clearly on at least one public act of robbing the rich (William Randolph Hearst, Jr.) in order to give to the poor (by blackmailing him into distributing food to them). It was similar to traditional social banditry not only in treating such redistribution as symbolic[†] and in concentrating primarily on individual wrong-righting – freeing individuals from jail appeals to political strong-arm groups – but in the brevity of its career. Other such activist groups, emerging out of the ashes of the worldwide student ferment of the late sixties, have also demonstrated a taste

[*] For the concept of 'primitive rebels', see my book of the same name (New York: Norton, 1965) which is probably responsible for such currency as the term enjoys. I understand that some of the Berkeley rebels of the 1960s claim to have recognized themselves in the social bandits and others described in that book, which was read by the more academically minded left.

[†] When it was pointed out that their demand would be beyond Hearst's finances, they answered, 'It was never intended that you feed the whole state . . . So whatever you come up with basically is OK.' John Bryan, *This Soldier Still At War* (New York/London, 1975). My information about the SLA is derived from this book, to which my friend, the late Ralph Gleason, drew my attention.

for operations which Jesse James would have understood, notably 'expropriation' (see Chapter 9), which therefore reached epidemic proportions in the 1970s and 1980s. However, unlike other such plunges into political outlawry, the SLA was unattached to any wider revolutionary organization, strategy, theory or movement, and the neo-primitivism of its home-grown thoughts and actions is therefore more obvious.

Traditional bandits were based on kin, neighbourhood and community. The Symbionese were unattached individuals by origin, none of whom had known or heard of each other until they met in the subcultural ghetto of the East Bay, as pebbles meet on a lowland sandbank, having been swept downstream along some complicated river-system. Though most of the eleven chief members of the group belonged to a sort of student intelligentsia, they were not in fact united by that common catalyst of revolutionary groups emerging from student life, the bonds which link contemporaries studying in the same university or faculty. Berkeley-Oakland was simply a place they gravitated to, wherever they had originally studied.

They lived less in a community – except in the purely geographical sense – than in an ambience of escape from 'bourgeois' values, a Latin Quarter or Montmartre, brought together by the informal shifting sociability of street, lodging, demo or party, by the common lifestyle of a *bohème*, by the common rhetoric of a dissident subculture which saw itself as revolutionary, and by sexual attraction – probably the strongest single factor bringing together this particular group of people. Hence women, usually irrelevant to or disruptive of traditional bandit units, were the essential (hetero or homo) cement of this one. The only model of a genuine mini-community, apart from memories of the bourgeois family, was 'the commune' and the small, tight, intense groups of revolutionary activists, of which several developed, by fission rather than combination, on the margins of campus mobilization. The political phraseology of the SLA came mainly from these.

Again, traditional primitive rebels are united by a common and inherited set of values and beliefs about society so strong as hardly to need, or to be capable of, formal articulation. They only needed to be applied. But except for the vocabulary of the Declaration of Independence, which still echoes through the manifestoes of the group, these neo-primitives had no such common stock of ideas. They had to translate their personal experience of alienation into a formalized ideology, or rather rhetoric, made up of a confused selection of phrases from the revolutionary dictionary of the 'new left' and Californian orientalism and psychobabble. It took the form of shadowy exercises in manifesto oratory, coming close to practice only in a few negative demands – the abolition of prisons, the abolition of 'the rent system of exploitation' in houses and apartments – and the call for a system 'that will neither force people into nor force them to stay in personal relationships that they do not wish to be in'.* It was a cry of lost people against a cruel and atomized society, but it provided them only with a justification for symbolic gestures of violence, an assertion of their existence as people to whom attention should be paid through their reflection in the magnifying mirror of the media, and a legitimation for the lifestyle of the small illegal activist group which was their substitute for community and society. The members were personally 'reborn' in the group, chose new names, and evolved a private symbolism.

Illegality as free personal choice, illegal acts abstracted from social and political reality: these, therefore, distinguish the

*Bryan, *This Soldier Still At War*, p. 312. The book contains a collection of the SLA documents.

traditional social bandit from his latter-day imitators or equivalents. Most people in this book did not *choose* outlawry (except, where banditry was an established way of earning a living, as a professional career). They were forced into it by what neither they nor their society regarded as a criminal act, and the rest followed. The most that one might argue is that tough kids who were unlikely to take injustice or offence lying down, were also more than likely to get into this sort of trouble. That links the traditional social bandits to people like the black prisoners, who certainly were among the inspirations and models of groups like the SLA, though the society which brands a large proportion of its black subproletariat with the mark of jail and jail experience has very little in common with that which produced its small fringe of *cangaçeiros* or haiduks. Nevertheless, though the SLA and no doubt other similar and politically more serious groups may contain a few people of this kind – and may indeed, in their search for popular roots and ideological legitimation, make great efforts to include the token blacks, chicanos or proletarians – the bulk of their members are drawn from an entirely different social constituency. They are the sons and daughters of the middle classes (however locally defined), and often, though hardly in the case of the SLA, of the upper middle classes. The institutions in Argentina decimated by the terrorism with which the military destroyed the armed insurrectionaries were the upper forms of the elite high schools. Such activists have freely chosen outlawry. The most that one can say is that in the 1960s and 1970s, for reasons which are not the concern of this book, this free choice was more likely to be made by sons and daughters of the middle classes and elites. They did not have to any more than the young Friedrich Engels had to become a communist.

Again, the traditional social bandit's actions, whether

professional or 'political', are part of the fabric of his society and, in a sense, derive logically from it. Much of this book has been devoted to showing how this is so. Indeed, as I have argued, they are so enmeshed in that fabric that they are not, in fact, revolutionaries, though they may become so in certain circumstances. Their actions may have symbolic value, but they are not directed against symbols but against specific and, as it were, organic, targets: not 'the system' but the Sheriff of Nottingham. There are, especially among highly sophisticated and politically informed terrorist groups, occasional coups against specific victims from which specific results are expected, such as the killing of Carrero Blanco by the Basque ETA or the kidnapping and murder of Aldo Moro by the Italian Red Brigades. In such cases the very sophistication of the political calculations behind the coups, implying as it does a very high degree of information about top-level national politics, removes the perpetrators far from the sphere in which social banditry, old or new, operates.*

On the other hand, in most cases the lists of possible victims sometimes discovered in the papers of captured neo-Robin Hoods, including the SLA, are arbitrary, except insofar as they pursue that private cops-and-robbers war, concerned primarily with the defence, protection and liberation of arrested and imprisoned comrades, by which – for psychological reasons – the activities of such groups tend to be increasingly monopolized. They have only an increasingly indirect relation to the ostensible political objects of the groups. Otherwise, since they are essentially symbols of 'the

---

* Thus the calculation that Aldo Moro's disappearance might destroy the chances of establishing a 'historic compromise' between the Demochristian and Communist parties, of which he was said to be the chief Demochristian champion, is one which would be made in Italy only by professional top-level politicians or intellectuals steeped in the sort of subtleties which fill the columns of parliamentary journalism and are of little interest to the mass of Italians, even when comprehensible to them.

system', other possible victims could be easily substituted for those actually chosen: another banker for the late Ponto, another industrialist for the late Schleyer, victims of the 'Red Army Fraction'. Moreover, in the case of such symbolic victims, no specific political consequence is expected to follow the action other than a public assertion of the presence and power of the revolutionaries, and the presence of their cause.

At this point there is a similarity between the old bandits and the new activists, though it underlines the fundamental difference in their social contexts. In both cases 'the myth' is a primary object of the action. For the classical bandit it is its own reward, for the neo-bandits its value lies in the supposed propagandist consequences, and in any case, by the nature of such illegal groups, it has to be a collective myth, the individuals usually remaining anonymous.[*] Yet in both cases what we would today call 'publicity' is of the essence. Without it, bandits or groups would have no public existence. Yet the nature of public existence is fundamentally changed by the appearance of the mass media. The classical bandits established their reputation by direct contact with their constituency and the grapevine of an oral society. They entered the primitive equivalent of the mass media, ballads, chapbooks and the like, only once they had established it. Some of those discussed in this book have never made the transition from face-to-face and oral reputation to the wider myth – e.g. (so far as one can tell), Maté Cosido in the Argentine Chaco. There is a late stage in the history of social banditry when something like modern mass media already catch and diffuse the bandit myth: probably in the Australia

[*] It is almost invariably the authorities or opponents of the group who put names to anonymous actions – e.g. who personalized the 'Red Army Fraction' as the 'Baader-Meinhof gang'. How far the nameless people thus given names get satisfaction from their public reputation is another question.

of Ned Kelly, the USA of Jesse James, possibly in twentieth-century Sardinia (though the celebrated bandits of the region like Pasquale Tanteddu, in spite of their penchant for publicity, acquired fame outside their region only through and among intellectuals), certainly in the era of Bonnie and Clyde. Still, celebrity in the media remained, by and large, an additional bonus on top of the just reward of bandit fame.

Today the media are overwhelmingly the dominant, perhaps the only, creators of the myth. Moreover, they have the power to give instant and, in the right circumstances, worldwide exposure such as no previous era of history could possess. (Warhol's utopia of a moment's 'celebrity' for every citizen could not have been formulated in a non-media world.) The media-created myth may have the drawback of built-in impermanence, being the creation of an economy geared to disposable souls as well as to disposable beer cans, but this can be offset by repeating the actions which ensure media exposure. In this respect the traditional bandit tortoise may actually beat the electric hare of his successors. Nobody ever asks 'Whatever happened to Jesse James?' Many, even today, have to be reminded who Patty Hearst was. Nevertheless, the Symbionese Liberation Army established its brief celebrity with a speed and on a scale which, while it lasted, far surpassed that of the live Jesse James.

The political image and effectiveness of neo-Robin Hoods is therefore achieved not through their actions as such, but through their success in making headlines, and they are planned primarily to achieve this object. Hence the paradox that some of the actions by which the classical bandit would expect to build his myth are those which his successors prefer not to advertise, because they would create the wrong image (e.g. that of the criminal as distinct from the political militant). The bulk of the ransom-kidnappings and bank robberies by which militants accumulate the often very substantial funds for their, under present circumstances, often very expensive mode of operation, almost certainly remain anonymous and indistinguishable from any other professional robberies or kidnappings, in spite of the publicity value of attacks on the rich.* Few 'expropriations' are advertised as the work of such groups, unless specific political points can be made by doing so – e.g. the revelation of shady dealings by prominent depositors. (The Tupamaros in Uruguay were skilled in thus 'politicizing' bank-raids while distracting attention from the actual content of the action, which was robbery.)

Conversely, such actions don't acquire publicity because they are directed against targets accepted by the general public as 'enemies of the people', though political activists often choose them on those grounds. The name of William Randolph Hearst, a target of the SLA, may still produce a *frisson* among an older generation of US radicals and perhaps intellectual movie-buffs, but the fact that Ponto was a prominent banker and Schleyer a representative spokesman of industrial capital almost certainly did not gain the Red Army Fraction any sympathy in West Germany except

---

* Genuinely popular activists may not entirely resist the Robin Hood instinct even then, but, as it were, privately. Thus a working-class militant, returning from a bank-raid to an illegal 'safe house': 'Just in front of the apartment . . . there's this beggar with his hat in his hand and asks me, have I got money. "Man," I say, "have I got it!" So I pour all the small change in his hat, there's so much it spills on the street, and that guy, all he can say is "A long life to you, you're the best man in the world," and I say to him "Man, I'm having a good time. Life is simple, all you have to do is be in the right place at the right time. I've just been lucky that way, now it's happening to you, take it easy." And then I walk on.' (Bommi Bauman, *Wie Alles Anfing*, Munich, 1975, p. 105). This book, strongly critical of the Red Army Fraction, is a valuable guide to the rock-, blues- and hash-conditioned subculture of declassed and marginal youth out of which something not dissimilar to an old anarchist-bohemian milieu can grow. But Baumann is untypical of the West German 'urban guerrilla' scene and, as his book shows, knows himself to be untypical.

among the very restricted circles who already sympathized with such small-group armed action. Perhaps the attacks on policemen may still achieve some such effect. However, headlines may equally well be achieved by attacks on entirely neutral or uninvolved persons – athletes during the Munich Olympics of 1972 or drinkers at English pubs killed by IRA bombs – or against persons who, while regarded as suitable targets for esoteric group purposes (e.g. police informers) are merely John Does for the remainder of the population. And to the extent that the actual targets of action thus become incidental and arbitrary casualties in someone else's war, the similarity between old and new 'social banditry' is attenuated. All that remains is the demonstration that small groups of nameless outlaws, known only by abstract or meaningless titles or initials, are challenging the official structures of power and law.*

It is not part of the purpose of this book to consider the political effectiveness or to assess the theoretical and other justifications which have been put forward for the current revival of individual and small-group armed actions. My object here is simply to note the similarities and differences between them and 'social banditry' and their relation to its tradition, heritage and mode of action. There is some relation, though only one or two of the groups of this kind, in general (except the neo-anarchist†) those furthest removed from the most influential orthodoxies of revolutionary ideology, strategy and organization, show any marked characteristics of neo-primitivism. For the purposes of this study of classical social banditry, the relation is marginal,

---

* These observations naturally do not apply to movements which can be properly described as urban or rural popularly based guerrilla movements such as, e.g., the Provisional IRA in the Catholic areas of Ulster.

† It is worth observing that there appears to be virtually no direct and historical continuity between such neo-anarchist groups and the tiny survivals of the old anarchists to be found anywhere by 1968.

perhaps tangential. The exploration of these phenomena may be left to students of capitalist society in the late twentieth century. On the other hand, the *direct* continuation of the myths and traditions of classical social banditry in the modern industrial world is relevant to the purpose of this book.

In some ways, it is still alive. In the late 1970s an enthusiastic and militant Mexican reader of this author's *Primitive Rebels*, whose chapter on banditry has been expanded into the present book, encouraged the activists of a peasant movement in the north-east of that country to read that work. I refrain from speculating what his object was. The militants of the *Campamiento Tierra y Libertad* thought, perhaps not unnaturally, that the book was hard going. They did not understand much of it, and they could not see the point of much of what they read. But there was one part of it they did understand and that made sense to them: the part about social bandits. I mention this tribute from an unexpected and unintended public not only because it is the sort of experience which makes an author feel good, but because the inhabitants of the Huasteca Potosina region may be regarded as a qualified, competent, and no doubt, in the past, an experienced body of critics and commentators on the subject. It does not prove that the analysis put forward in *Bandits* is right. But it may give readers of the book some confidence that it is more than an exercise in antiquarianism or in academic speculation. Robin Hood, even in his most traditional forms, still means something in today's world, to people like these Mexican peasants. There are many of them. And they should know.

Notes

* * *

Preface

1 William Doyle, 'Feuds and Law and Order', *London Review of Books*, 14 Sep. 1989, p. 12.
2 Cf. E. J. Hobsbawm, Introduction to G. Ortalli, ed., *Bande Armate, Banditi, Banditismo e repressione di giustizia negli stati europei di antico regime* (Rome, 1986), p. 16.

Chapter 1: **Bandits, States and Power (pp. 7–18)**

1 G. C. Croce, *Barzeletta sopra la morte di Giacomo del Gallo famosissimo bandito* (Bologna, 1610), vv. 26–9, 131–54.
2 Giovanni Cherubini, 'La tipologia del bandito nel tardo medioevo', in Ortalli, op. cit., p. 353.
3 Fikret Adanir, 'Heiduckentum und osmanische Herrschaft: Sozial-geschichtlichte Aspekte der Diskussion um das frühneuzeitliche Räuberwesen in Südosteuropa', *Südost-Forschungen*, XLI, 1982, pp. 43–116.
4 See Gonzalo Sanchez and Donny Meertens, *Bandoleros, gamonales y campesinos: el caso de la Violencia en Colombia* (Bogotà, 1983) and my Preface to this work.
5 Antonio Pigliaru, *Il Banditismo in Sardegna: La vendetta barbaricina* (Varese, 1975), p. 419.
6 Bronislaw Geremek, 'Il pauperismo nell'eta pre-industriale', *Einaudi Storia 'Italia'*, vol. V (Turin, 1973), p. 695.
7 Billy Jaynes Chandler, *The Bandit King: Lampião of Brazil* (Texas A&M Univ. Press, 1978). I cite from the Portuguese edition (Rio de Janeiro, 1981), p. 27.
8 Phil Billingsley, *Bandits in Republican China* (Stanford, CA, 1988), p. 20. See also p. 16: 'Poverty . . . always lurked at the back of the perennial bandit presence, and starvation gave a powerful impetus to outlawry. A bandit captured in Sichuan, for example, told his army interrogator that the reason for his becoming a bandit could be found in his stomach if

they cared to cut him open. The intrigued official did just that after the execution: the stomach was found to contain nothing but grass.'

9 Hugo Chumbita, 'El bandido Artigas', *Todo Es Historia*, no. 356 (Buenos Aires, March 1997), pp. 8–27.

10 Fernand Braudel, *The Mediterranean and the Mediterranean World in the Age of Philip II* (Paris, 1949–orig. edn).

11 P. Imbs, ed., *Trésor de la langue française*, vol. 4 (Paris, 1975), v. 'brigand'; J. Corominas, *Diccionario Etimológico de la Lengua Castellana*, vol. 1 (Berne, 1954), v. Bando II (London, 1992 edn, Part II, 5.3), cited in Luigi Lacchè, *Latrocinium. Giustizia, scienza penale e repressione del banditismo in antico regime* (Milan, 1988), p. 45.

12 Karen Barkey, *Bandits and Bureaucrats: The Ottoman Route to State Centralization* (Ithaca/London, 1994), pp. 153–4.

13 'Aristocratic (despotic) empires were characteristically squeeze operations: when the elites wanted more, they did not think in terms of gains or productivity . . . They simply pressed and oppressed harder, and usually found some hidden juice. Sometimes they miscalculated and squeezed too hard, and that could mean flight, riot and opportunities for rebellion.' David S. Landes, *The Wealth and Poverty of Nations* (New York/London, 1998), p. 32.

14 See Daniele Marchesini, 'Banditi e identità', in G. Ortalli, op. cit., pp. 471–8.

15 Brent D. Shaw, 'Bandits in the Roman Empire', *Past & Present*, 105, 1984, pp. 3–52.

Chapter 2: **What is Social Banditry? (pp. 19–33)**

1 Molise, quoted in F. Molfese, *Storia del brigantaggio dopo l'unità* (Milan, 1964), p. 131.

2 Enrique Morselli-Sante De Sanctis, *Biografia de un bandito, Giuseppe Musolino di fronte alla psichiatria e alla sociologia. Studio medico-legale e considerazioni* (Milan, 1903), cited in L. Lombardi Satriani and M. Meligrana eds., *Diritto Egemone e Diritto Popolare: La Calabria negli studi di demologia giuridica* (Vibo Valentia, 1975) p. 478.

3 Carlos Miguel Ortiz Sarmiento, *La Violence en Colombie* (Paris, 1990), p. 205, n. 70. For an earlier estimate, G. Guzman, O. Fals Borda, E. Umaña Luna, *La Violencia en Colombia* (Bogotà 1964), vol. II, pp. 287–97.

4 *Le brigandage en Macédoine: Un rapport confidentiel au gouvernment bulgare* (Berlin, 1908), p. 38; information from Professor D. Dakin of Birkbeck College.

5 Stephen Wilson, *Feuding, Conflict and Banditry in Nineteenth Century Corsica* (Cambridge, 1988), pp. 5, 336.

6 Gaetano Cingari, *Brigantaggio, proprietai e contadini nel sud (1799–1900)* (Reggio Calabria, 1976), p. 141.

7 D. Eeckhoute, 'Les brigands en Russie du dix-septième au dix-neuvième siècle', in *Revue d'Histoire Moderne et Contemporaine*, XII, 1965, pp. 174–5.

8 E. Alabaster, *Notes and commentaries on the Chinese criminal law* (Luzac & Co.), pp. 400–2.

9 E. Lopez Albujar, *Los caballeros del delito* (Lima, 1936), pp. 75–6.

10 W. Crooke, *The Tribes and Castes of the North-West Provinces and Oudhe* (Calcutta, 1896), 4 vols, I, p. 49.

11 F. Molfese, op. cit., p. 130.

12 M. I. P. de Queiroz, *Os Cangaçeiros: Les bandits d'honneur brésiliens* (Paris, 1968), pp. 142, 164.

13 R. Rowland, '"Cantadores" del nordeste brasileño', in *Aportes*, 3 Jan. 1967, p. 138. For the real relations between this bandit and the holy man, which were rather more *nuancés*, cf. E. de Lima, *O mundo estranho dos cangaçeiros* (Salvador Bahia, 1965), pp. 113–14, and O. Anselmo, *Padre Cicero* (Rio de Janeiro, 1968).

Chapter 3: **Who becomes a Bandit? (pp. 34–45)**

1 Autobiography in G. Rosen, *Die Balkan-Haiduken* (Leipzig, 1878), p. 78.

2 F. Molfese, op. cit., pp. 127–8.

3 Phil Billingsley, *Bandits in Republican China* (Stanford, 1988), pp. 75–6

4 Information from Dr Eduardo Pizarro. For statistics see Carlos Miguel Ortiz Sarmiento, *La Violence en Colombie: Racines historiques et sociales* (Paris, 1990), p. 192, n. 45.

5 Hobsbawm, E. J., *Primitive Rebels* (Manchester University Press, 1959); Lopez Albujar, op. cit., p. 126.

6 Alejandro Franco, 'El Aymara del siglo XX', in *Amauta* (Lima) 23, 1929, p. 88.

7 Based on F. Molfese, op. cit., pp. 367–82.

8 A. H. Smith, *Village life in China* (New York/Chicago/Toronto, 1899), pp. 213–17.

9 F. C. B. Avé-Lallemant, *Das deutsche Gaunerthum* (Leipzig, 1858–62), II, p. 91n.

10 For details, G. Kraft, *Historische Studien zu Schillers Schauspiel 'Die Räuber'* (Weimar, 1959).

11 F. C. B. Avé-Lallemant, op. cit., I, p. 241. For confirmation of the differences between criminals and bandits from a medico-legal expert with experience of both, E. de Lima, op. cit., *passim*; G. Sangnier, *Le brigandage dans le Pas-de-Calais* (Blangermont, 1962), pp. 172, 196.

Chapter 4: **The Noble Robber (pp. 46–62)**

1 Pearl Buck (transl.), *All Men Are Brothers* (New York, 1937), p. 1258.
2 E. Morselli and S. de Sanctis, *Biografia di un bandito: Giuseppe Musolino, di fronte alla psichiatra ed alla sociologia*, (Milan n.d.), p. 175.
3 C. Bernaldo de Quiros, *El bandolerismo en España y Mexico* (Mexico, 1959), p. 59.
4 M. Pavlovich, 'Zelim Khan et le brigandage au Caucase' in *Revue du monde musulman*, XX, 1912, pp. 144, 146.
5 V. Zapata Cesti, *La delincuencia en el Peru* (Lima n.d.), p. 175.
6 M. L. Guzman, *The Memoirs of Pancho Villa* (Austin, TX, 1965), p. 8.
7 Alberto Carrillo Ramirez, *Luis Pardo, 'El Gran Bandido'* (Lima, 1970), pp. 117–18, 121.
8 Miguel Barnet, *Cimarrón* (Havana, 1967), pp. 87–8.
9 R. V. Russell, *The Tribes and Castes of the Central Provinces of India* (Macmillan, 1916), 4 vols, I, p. 60; Charles Hervey, *Some Records of Crime* (Simpson, 1892), I, p. 331.
10 Kent L. Steckmesser, 'Robin Hood and the American outlaw', in *Journal of American Folklore*, 79, April–June 1966, p. 350.
11 P. Buck (trans.), op. cit., p. 328.
12 J. Martinez-Alier, *La Estabilidad del latifundismo* (Paris, 1968), chs 1–6.
13 J. Caro Baroja, *Ensayo sobre la leteratura de Cordel* (Madrid, 1969), p. 375.
14 A. v. Schweiger-Lerchenfeld, *Bosnien* (Vienna, 1878), p. 122; P. Bourde, *En Corse* (Paris, 1887), pp. 218–19.
15 I take all this information from Douglas Dakin's *The Greek Struggle in Macedonia* (Salonika, 1966).
16 F. Kanitz, *La Bulgarie danubienne* (Paris, 1882), p. 346.
17 Special number on Calabria of *Il Ponte*, 1950, p. 1305.
18 Juan Regla Campistol and Joan Fuster, *El bandolerisme català* (Barcelona, 1963), II, p. 35.
19 D. H. Meijer, 'Over het bendewezen op Java', in *Indonesie* III, 1949–50, p. 183; W. Crooke, loc. cit., p. 47. See also Nertan Macedo, *Capitão Virgulino Ferreira da Silva: Lampiao*, 2nd edn (Rio de Janeiro, 1968), p. 96.
20 Ivan Olbracht, *Der Räuber Nikola Schuhaj* (East Berlin, 1953), p. 100.
21 C. G. Harper, *Half-hours with the Highwaymen* (London, 1908), II, p. 235.

Chapter 5: **The Avengers (pp. 63–76)**

1 Antonio Teodoro dos Santos, *O poeta Garimpeiro*, 'Lampiao, king of the bandits', chapbook (Saõ Paulo, 1959).
2 N. Macedo, op. cit., p. 183.

3 Cf. Paris Lozano, 'Los guerilleros del Tolima', in *Revista de las Indias* (Bogotà, 1936), I, no. 4, p. 31.
4 Yashar Kemal, *Mehmed My Hawk* (Collins, 1961), p. 56.
5 Guzman, Fals Borda, Umaña Luna, op. cit., I, p. 182.
6 Ibid., II, pp. 327–8.
7 Ivan Olbracht, *Berge und Jahrhunderte* (East Berlin, 1952), pp. 82–3.

Chapter 6: **Haiduks (pp. 77–90)**

1 From A. Dozon, *Chansons populaires bulgares inédites* (Paris, 1875), p. 208.
2 A. Strausz, *Bulgarische Volksdichtungen* (Vienna/Leipzig, 1895), pp. 295–7.
3 *Le brigandage en Macédoine*, loc. cit., p. 37. For the absence of homosexuality among Brazilian bandits, E. de Lima, op cit., p. 45.
4 A. Dozon, op. cit., p. 184.
5 J. Baggalay, *Klephtic Ballads* (Blackwell, 1936), pp. 18–19; C. J. Jireček, *Geschichte der Bulgaren* (Prague, 1876), p. 474.
6 J. C. V. Engel, *Staatskunde und Geschichte von Dalmatien, Croatien und Slavonien* (Halle, 1798), p. 232.
7 Marko Fedorowitsch, *Die Slawen der Türkei* (Dresden/Leipzig, 1844), II, p. 206.

Chapter 7: **The Economics and Politics of Banditry (pp. 91–105)**

1 J. Usang Ly, in *Journal of Race Development*, 8, 1917–18, p. 370.
2 Leonardo Mota, *No tempo de Lampião* (Rio de Janeiro, 1968 edn), pp. 55–6.
3 M. I. P. de Queiroz, op. cit., pp. 9–10.
4 Billingsley, op. cit., pp. 163–77, for ransom procedures. Citations on p. 163 and quoting Aleko E. Lilius, *I Sailed with Chinese Pirates* (London, 1930), p. 135.
5 L. Mota, op. cit., p. 54.
6 R. V. Russell, op. cit., I, pp. 52–3; III, pp. 237–9, 474.
7 See O. Anselmo, op. cit., pp. 528–36.
8 See Teniente Coronel (R) Genaro Matos, *Operaciones irregulares al norte de Cajamarca 1924–5 a 1927* (Lima, 1968).
9 Romulo Merino Arana, *Historia policial del Peru* (Lima n.d.), pp. 177–8; G. Matos, op. cit., pp. 390–8.
10 G. Matos, op. cit., p. 75; cited from Salamón Vilchez Murga, *Fusiles y Machetes*, a local source.
11 D. Eeckhoute, loc. cit., pp. 201–2.

Chapter 8: **Bandits and Revolutions (pp. 106–19)**

1 J. Delumeau, *Vie économique et sociale de Rome dans la seconde moitié du seizième siècle* (Paris, 1957–9), II, p. 557.
2 P. M. van Wulfften-Palthe, *Psychological Aspects of the Indonesian Problem* (Leiden, 1949), p. 32.
3 J. Koetschet, *Aus Bosniens letzter Türkenzeit* (Vienna/Leipzig, 1905), pp. 6–8.
4 *District Gazetteers of the United Provinces* (Allahabad, 1911), I, p. 185.
5 Sartono Kartodirdjo, *The Peasants' Revolt of Banten in 1888* (The Hague, 1966), p. 23.
6 Wulfften-Palthe, op. cit., p. 34.
7 M. Pavlovich, loc. cit., pp. 146, 159.
8 Cf. M. L. Guzman, op. cit. See also Friedrich Katz, *The Life and Times of Pancho Villa* (Stanford, CA, 1999), pp. 73, 101.
9 Stuart Schram, *Mao Tse-tung* (Harmondsworth, 1966), p. 43.
10 See the superb chapter 'Bandits and the Revolutionary Movement' in P. Billingsley, op. cit., pp. 226–70.
11 Luis Gonzalez, *Pueblo en vilo* (Mexico DF, 1968), p. 251.

Chapter 9: **The Expropriators (pp. 120–38)**

1 A fuller life of him has since been written: Antonio Tellez, *Sabaté, Guerrilla Extraordinary* (London, 1974). See also the same author's *La guerrilla urbana I: Facerias* (Paris, 1974).
2 E. Lister, 'Lessons of the Spanish Guerrilla War (1939–51)' in *World Marxist Review*, 8, II, 1965, pp. 53–8; Tomas Cossias, *La lucha contra el 'Maquis' en España* (Madrid, 1956).

Chapter 10: **The Bandit as Symbol (pp. 139–45)**

1 A. J. Paterson, *The Magyars: Their Country and Institutions* (London, 1869), I, p. 213.
2 I. Olbracht, *Berge and Jahrhunderte*, p. 113.
3 I. Olbracht, *Der Räuber Nikola Schuhaj*, pp. 76–7.

Appendix A: **Women and Banditry (pp. 146–9)**

1 *Diario de un guerillero Latinamericano* (Montevideo, 1968), p. 60.
2 Ibid., pp. 60–1.
3 M. I. P. de Queiroz, op. cit., p. 179.
4 Ibid., p. 183.
5 C. J. Jireček, op. cit., p. 476.
6 V. Zapata Cesti, op. cit., pp. 205–6.

7 In R. Merino Arana, op. cit.

8 Hugo Nario, *Mesías y bandoleros pampeanos* (Buenos Aires, 1993), pp. 115–17.

9 Julio Caro Baroja discusses them in *Ensayo sobre la Leteratura de Cordel* (Madrid, 1969), pp. 389–90.

Appendix B: **The Bandit Tradition (pp. 150–66)**

1 F. Katz, op. cit., p. 830.

2 'The Bandit Giuliano', in E. J. Hobsbawm, *Uncommon People: Resistance, Rebellion and Jazz* (London, 1998), pp. 191–9.

3 See Xavier Torres I Sans, *Els bandolers (s. XVI–XVII)* (Vic, 1991, Cap. V).

4 J. C. Holt, *Robin Hood* (London, 1982), esp. pp. 154–5.

5 Hugo Chumbita, 'Alias Maté Cosido', *Todo Es Historia*, no. 293 (Buenos Aires), Nov. 1991, pp. 82–95.

6 Gaetano Cingari, *Brigantaggio, proprietari e contadini nel Sud (1799–1900)*, (Reggio Calabria, 1976), pp. 205–66.

7 Dr Andrzej Emeryk Mankowski has kindly provided me with an English version of his fascinating 'Legenda Salapatka – "Orla"', based on fieldwork by the Ethnology and Cultural Anthropology Dept of Warsaw University in 1988–90.

8 Antonio Escudero Gutierrez, 'Jaime "El Barbudo": un ejempeo de bandolerismo social', *Estudis d'història contemporània del país Valencià*, no. 3, University of Valencia, Dept of Contemporary History (Valencia, 1982), pp. 57–88.

9 Xavier Costa Clavell, *Bandolerismo, Romerias y jergas gallegas* (La Coruña, 1980), pp. 75–90.

10 Joseph Ritson, *Robin Hood: A Collection of All the Ancient Poems, Songs and Ballads now Extant* (London, 1795, 1832, 1887).

11 Uwe Danker, *Räuberbanden im Alten Reich um 1700: Ein Beitrag zur Geschichte von Herrschaft und Kriminalität in der frühen Neuzeit* (Frankfurt, 1988), I, p. 474.

12 P. Billingsley, op. cit., pp. 2, 4, 51.

13 *Figures de la gueuserie: Textes présentés par Roger Chartier* (Paris, 1982), pp. 83–96.

14 Maria Luciana Buseghin and Walter Corelli, 'Ipotesi per l'interpretazione del banditismo in Umbria nel primo decennio dell'Unità', *Istituto 'Alcide Cervi' Annali*, 2/1980, pp. 265–80.

15 Torres I Sans, op. cit., pp. 206, 216; C. Bernaldo de Quirós and Luís Ardila, *El Bandolerismo Andaluz* (Madrid, 1978; original edition, 1933), *passim*; A. Escudero Gutierrez, op. cit., p. 73.

16 Felix Molina Tellez, *El mito la leyenda y el hombre. Usos y costumes del folklore* (Buenos Aires, 1947), cited in Hugo Nario, *Mesías y bandoleros*

pampanos (Buenos Aires, 1993), pp. 125–6; Hugo Chumbita, 'Bandoleros sanctificados', *Todo Es Historia*, no. 340 (Buenos Aires), Nov. 1995, pp. 78–90.

17 Yves Castan, 'L'image du brigand au XVIIIe siècle dans le Midi de la France', in G. Ortalli, ed., op. cit., p. 346.

18 Richard Gillespie, *Soldiers of Peron: The Montoneros* (New York, 1982), chap. 2.

19 I follow the ideas of Gonzalo Sanchez and Donny Meertens, first hinted at in their *Bandoleros, gamonales y campesinos*, p. 239. See also, in English, 'Political Banditry and the Colombian *Violencia*', in Richard W. Slatta, ed., *Bandidos: The Varieties of Latin American Banditry* (Westport, CT, 1987), p. 168.

20 Nicolé Girón, *Heraclio Bernal: Bandolero, cacique o precursor de la revolucion?* (Mexico DF, INAH, 1976).

21 Allen L. Woll, 'Hollywood Bandits 1910–1981', in R. Slatta, ed., op. cit., pp. 171–80.

22 Linda Lewin, 'Oral Tradition and Elite Myth: The Legend of Antônio Silvino in Brazilian Popular Culture', *Journal of Latin American Lore*, 5:2, 1979, pp. 57–204.

23 Gonzalo Sanchez, Prologue to Maria Isaura Pereira de Queiroz, *Os Cangaçeiros: La epopeya bandolera del Nordeste de Brasil* (Bogotà, 1992), pp. 15–16; see also L. Lewin, loc. cit., p. 202.

24 G. Sanchez and D. Meertens, 1987, p. 168.

25 P. Billingsley, op. cit., p. 133.

Postscript (pp. 167–99)

1 Anton Blok, 'The Peasant and the Brigand: Social Banditry Reconsidered', *Comparative Studies in Society and History*, 14, 1972, pp. 495–504. For the most mature statement, A. Blok, *The Mafia of a Sicilian Village: A Study of Violent Peasant Entrepreneurs 1860–1960* (Oxford, 1974), pp. 97–102.

2 A. Blok, 1974, pp. 99–101.

3 E. J. Hobsbawm, Introduction to Ortalli, ed., op. cit., p. 15.

4 *Leben und Ende des berüchtigten Anführers einer Wildchützenbande, Mathias Klostermayers, oder des sogenannten Bayerischen Hiesels* (Augsburg, 1772), pp. 155–60.

5 H. Chumbita, 1995, pp. 80–1.

6 J. C. Holt, op. cit.; L. Lewin, loc. cit., pp. 157–202.

7 See the remarks of Matei Cazacu in 'Dimensions de la révolte primitive en Europe centrale et orientale' (Débat ouvert le 5/VI/1981; President: Marc Ferro), *Questions et Débats sur l'Europe Centrale et Orientale*, no. 4, Dec. 1985, p. 91 (Paris, duplicated).

8 F. Adanir, op. cit., *passim*.

9 F. Katz, op. cit., cap. 1.

10 Spiros Asdrachas, in 'Dimensions de la révolte primitive en Europe centrale et orientale', p. 88.

11 Carsten Küther, *Räuber und Gauner in Deutschland: das organisierte Bandenwesen im 18. und frühen 19. Jahrhundert* (Göttingen, 1983).

12 Anton Blok, *De Bokkerijders: Roversbanden en geheime Genootschappen in de Landen van Overmaas [1730–1744]* (Amsterdam, 1991). A. Blok, 'The *Bokkerijders*: Eighteenth-century Brigandage in the Meuse Valley', in G. Ortalli, ed., op. cit., pp. 363–4.

13 On this distinction, see K.-S. Kramer, 'Ehrliche und Unehrliche Gewerbe', in A. Erler et al., eds., *Handwörterbuch zur deutschen Rechtsgeshichte* (Berlin, 1971), pp. 855–8; W. Dankert, *Unehrliche Leute* (Berne/Munich, 1963).

14 N. Castan, 'La Justice Expeditive', *Annales ESC*, 31/2, 1976; p. 338.

15 Ibid., p. 334.

16 Vance Randolph, *Ozark Mountain Folks* (New York, 1932), pp. 89, 91, quoted in James R. Green, *Grass-Roots Socialism: Radical Movements in the Southwest 1895–1943* (Baton Rouge/London, 1978), pp. 336–7.

17 J. R. Green, op. cit., pp. 339–42.

18 Ibid., p. 340.

19 David Moss, 'Bandits and Boundaries in Sardinia', *Man*, NS, vol. 14, 1979, pp. 477–96. See also John Day in B. Vincent, ed., *Les marginaux et les exclus dans l'histoire* (Paris, 1979), pp. 178–214.

20 Pat O'Malley, 'Social bandits, modern capitalism and the traditional peasantry: a critique of Hobsbawm', *Journal of Peasant Studies*, 6/4, 1979, pp. 489–99. See also *The Class Production of Crime: Banditry and Class Strategies in England and Australia* (mimeo, n.d.).

21 Don R. Bowen, 'Guerrilla War in Western Missouri, 1862–65', *Comparative Studies in History and Society*, 19, 1977, pp. 30–51.

22 Cf. Alberto Ledda, *La civiltá fuorilegge; natura e storia del banditismo sardo* (Milan, 1971), pp. 94–106. On the economics of Italian rural kidnapping in Calabria, see P. Arlacchi, 'The Mafia and Capitalism', *New Left Review*, no. 118, 1979, pp. 53–72 and esp. L. Ciconte, Ndrangheta dall 'unita a oggi (Bari, 1992), pp. 325–29.

Further Reading

***

Since the earlier editions of the present book the comparative study of the history of banditry has advanced notably, though mostly it remains regional rather than global. Much of this work arose from the numerous conferences and colloquia on bandit history which testify to the liveliness of the subject. The bibliography is immense, but, partly for linguistic reasons, I cannot claim adequate acquaintance with it outside Western and Central Europe and the Americas.

The earlier history of banditry, pioneered in Fernand Braudel's 'Misère et banditisme' (*Annales ESC*, 2/2, 1947) and in his great *The Mediterranean and the Mediterranean World in the Age of Philip II* (Paris, 1949 – orig. edn) has increasingly attracted attention.

For ancient banditry, Brent Shaw, 'Bandits in the Roman Empire' (*Past & Present*, 105, 1984, pp. 3–52), G. Ortalli, ed., *Bande Armate, Banditi, Banditismo e repressione di giustizia negli stati europei di antico regime* (Rome, 1986) and Fikret Adanir, 'Heiduckentum und osmanische Herrschaft: Sozialgeschichtliche Aspekte der Diskussion um das frühneuzeitliche Räuberwesen in Südosteuropa' (*Südost-Forschungen*, vol. XLI, Munich, 1982, pp. 43–116) between them cover almost all of Europe, except Russia and Poland. See also the important Karen Barkey, *Bandits and Bureaucrats: The Ottoman Route to State Centralization* (Ithaca/London, 1994), R. Villari 'Banditismo sociale alla fine del Cinquecento' in his *Ribelli e riformatori dal XVI al XVIII secolo* (Rome, 1979) and

P. Benadusi, 'Un bandito del '500: Marco Sciarra. Per uno studio sul banditismo al tempo de Sisto V' (*Studi Romani*, 1979). Perhaps equally relevant are the (mainly Italian) studies of the legal status and treatment of banditry. In addition to Ortalli, op cit., see D. Cavalca, *Il bando nella prassi e nella dottrina giuridica medievale* (Milan, 1978) and L. Lacchè, *Latrocinium. Giustizia, scienza penale e repressione del banditismo in antico regime* (Milan, 1988). Other relevant titles will be mentioned under their geographical headings.

National, regional and even local monographs continue to provide the bulk of the literature. With the exception of Latin America it is still dominated by the classic regions of banditry, the Mediterranean, East and South-east Europe. However, fortunately a body of important studies on CHINA is now available in English. Phil Billingsley, *Bandits in Republican China* (Stanford, CA, 1988) is basic, as is Jean Chesneaux, 'The Modern Relevance of Shui-hu Chuan: Its Influence on Rebel Movements in Nineteenth- and Twentieth-Century China' *(Papers on Far Eastern History*, 3, Canberra, Mar 1971, pp. 1–25). Jean Chesneaux, ed. *Popular Movements and Secret Societies in China 1840–1950* (Stanford, 1972) and Elizabeth J. Perry, *Rebels and Revolutionaries in North China 1845–1945* (Stanford, 1980) are also recommended.

Banditry in other parts of Asia is less well treated. On the Indian subcontinent the study of banditry, which figures in Hindu religious traditions, shows signs of activity. However, the monumental compilations of ethnographically-minded nineteenth-century imperial administrators (e.g. R. V. Russell, *The Tribes and Castes of Central India*, 4 vols, London, 1916) are still basic. Jacques Pouchepadass's chapter on the 'criminal tribes' in B. Vincent, ed., *Les marginaux et les exclus dans l'histoire* (Paris, 1979, pp. 122–54) is relevant. David Shulman discusses banditry in the name of the deity in

'On South Indian Bandits and Kings' (*Indian Economic and Social History Review*, vol. 17/3, Jul.-Sep. 1980, pp. 283–306). Amy Carmichael, *Raj, Brigand Chief: the true story of an Indian Robin Hood driven by persecution to dacoity: an account of his life of daring, feats of strength, escapes and tortures, his robbery of the rich and generosity to the poor . . . etc.* (London, 1927) is recommended to admirers of S. J. Perelman, as the only work about a bandit with Prefaces by three Anglican bishops and a member of the 1924 Mount Everest expedition ('a true story about a real sportsman – here it is'). Its historical value is less obvious. David Arnold, 'Dacoity and rural crime in Madras 1860–1940' (*Journal of Peasant Studies*, VI/2, 1979, pp. 140–67) holds that 'Hobsbawm's remarks about South Asia are unfortunate and misleading'. The subject has now begun to enter Indian commercial cinema.

Other Asian regions seem to have attracted less attention. In INDONESIA, or rather Java, there is Sartono Kartodirdjo, *The Peasant Revolt of Banten in 1888* (Leiden, 1966) and P. M. van Wulfften-Palthe, *Psychological Aspects of the Indonesian Problem* (Leiden, 1949). Cheah Boon Kheng has studied the subject in MALAYSIA: 'Hobsbawm's Social Banditry, Myth and Historical Reality: A Case in the Malaysian State of Kedah' (*Bulletin of Concerned Asian Scholars*, vol. 17/4, 1985, pp. 34–50), and *The Peasant Robbers of Kedah 1900–1929: Historical and Folk Perspectives* (Oxford University Press, Singapore, 1988). See also David B. Johnston, 'Bandit, *Nakleng*, and Peasant in Rural Thai Society' (*Contributions to Asian Studies*, vol. 15, 1980, pp. 90–101). Insofar as it deals largely with Anatolia, Karen Barkey op.cit. must also count as Asian.

Perhaps not surprisingly, given its history since the Cuban revolution, LATIN AMERICA has seen a more impressive growth in bandit historiography than any other part of the world. Richard Slatta, ed., *Bandidos: The Varieties of Latin*

American Banditry (Westport, CT, 1987) gives a continent-wide conspectus. See also Paul J. Vanderwood, 'Bandits in Nineteenth-Century Latin America: An Introduction to the Theme' (*Biblioteca Americana*, I, 2, Nov. 1982, pp 1–28) and the special issue edited by the same author, 'Social Banditry and Spanish American Independence 1790–1821' (*Biblioteca Americana* I, 2, Nov. 1982). BRAZIL and PERU, both with strongly established bandit traditions, which led the field in the early 1970s, are still ahead. For Brazil, the chief new works on the *cangaçeiros* come from Peter Singelmann, ('Political Structure and Social Banditry in Northeast Brazil', *Journal of Latin American Studies*, 7/1, 1975, pp. 59–83), Billy Jaynes Chandler, *The Bandit King: Lampião of Brazil* (Texas A&M Univ. Press, 1978) and the writings of Linda Lewin, notably 'The Oligarchical Limitations of Social Banditry in Brazil: The Case of the "Good" Thief Antônio Silvino' (*Past & Present*, 82, Feb. 1982, pp. 114–46). For Peru, E. Lopez Albujar, *Los caballeros del delito* (Lima, 1936, second edn 1973) remains a classic, but the more inaccessible local publications mentioned in some of my references, can now be supplemented by such works as Carlos Aguirre/Charles Walker, eds, *Bandoleros, abigeos y montoneros: criminalidad y violencia en el Peru, siglos XVIII–XX* (Lima, 1990) and Lewis Taylor, *Bandits and Politics in Peru: Landlord and Peasant Violence in Hualgayoc* (Cambridge, UK, 1986). For ARGEN-TINA, another country with a tendency to idealize its armed and lawless *gaucho* and *montonero* past, the notes in Richard Slatta's chapter in *Bandidos* provide a (sceptical) guide to banditry, but the chief chronicler of the subject is Hugo Chumbita, in a series of articles, not readily accessible to foreign readers, in the popular Buenos Aires review *Todo Es Historia*. Hugo Nario, *Mesias y bandoleros pampeanos* (Buenos Aires, 1993) is to the point. Gonzalo Sanchez and Donny Meertens, *Bandoleros, gamonales y campesinos: El caso de la*

Violencia en Colombia (Bogotà, 1984) and Carlos Miguel Ortiz Sarmiento, *La Violence en Colombie: Racines historiques et sociales* (Paris, 1990) – both with Prefaces by the present writer – are the best guides to the phenomenon in COLOMBIA, a country which – perhaps for reasons illuminated by both books – never developed a Robin Hood tradition. Erick D. Langer (in Richard Slatta, op. cit.) and Benjamin Orlove (in B. S. Orlove and G. Custard, eds, *Land and Power in Latin America*, New York/London, 1980) explore the terrain for BOLIVIA.

For MEXICO the traditional introduction is C. Bernaldo de Quirós, *El Bandolerismo en España y Mexico* (Mexico, 1959). Paul Vanderwood is the ranking expert in the field – *Disorder and Progress: Bandits, Police and Mexican Development* (Lincoln, NE, 1981) – but Friedrich Katz, *The Life and Times of Pancho Villa* (Stanford, 1999) is indispensable. On the interaction of revolution and banditry, see Samuel Brunk, 'The Sad Situation of Civilians and Soldiers': The Banditry of Zapatismo in the Mexican Revolution' (*American Historical Review*, vol. 101/2, April 1996, pp. 331–53). Not surprisingly, historical banditry in CUBA has attracted historians. The more unexpected patronage of these studies by the authorities of the Canary Islands (Manuel de Paz Sanchez, Jose Fernandez Fernandez, Nelson Lopez Novegil, *El Bandolerismo en Cuba 1800–1933*, 2 vols, Santa Cruz de Tenerife, 1993, 1994) is explained by the prominence of Canarian emigrants in Cuba. See also Prof. de Paz Sanchez, 'El bandolerismo social en Cuba (1881–1893)' in *IX Jornadas de Estudios Canarias-America: Las relaciones canario-cubanas'* (Santa Cruz de Tenerife, 1989, pp. 29–50). Probably more accessible is Rosalie Schwartz, *Lawless Liberators: Political Banditry and Cuban Independence* (Durham, NC/London, 1989). For the most famous of Cuban bandits, See Marie Poumier Tachequel, *Contribution à l'étude du banditime social à*

Cuba: L'histoire et le mythe de Manuel Garcia 'Rey de los Campos de Cuba' (1851–1895) (Paris, 1986).

Studies of banditry in AFRICA are not yet far advanced, although Charles van Onselen's explorations of urban low-life in South Africa throw much light on the problem. It is probably too early for any comprehensive study of the continent south of the Sahara.

EUROPEAN bandit studies have continued to advance.

For ITALY, whose *banditi* were long the most famous in literature and art, the monographic literature is probably still larger than for any other country. Most of it deals with the classic bandit regions of southern Italy and the islands. For the southern mainland, F. Molfese, *Storia del brigantaggio dopo l'unità* (Milan, 1964), esp. Chapter 3 Part I, Gaetano Cingari, *Brigantaggio, proprietari e contadini nel Sud (1799–1900)* (Reggio Calabria, 1976) and Enzo D'Alessandro, *Brigantaggio e Mafia in Sicilia* (Messina/Florence, 1959) as well as Anton Blok, *The Mafia of a Sicilian Village: A Study of Violent Peasant Entrepreneurs 1860–1960* (Oxford, 1974) remain important. Cingari contains sixty fundamental pages on the Calabrian bandit Musolino. For the persistence of a regional bandit tradition, see also A. Scirocco, 'Fenomeni di persistenza del ribellismo contadino: il brigantaggio in Calabria prima dell'Unità' (*Archivio Storico per le Provine Napoletane*, 3d ser. XX, 1981, pp. 245–79). The evolution of Sardinian banditry, which flared up in the late 1960s, is the subject of dispute among historians, social anthropologists and others. See Pietro Marongiu, *Introduzione allo studio del banditismo sociale in Sardegna* (Sassari, 1973), John Day, 'Banditisme et societe pastorale en Sardaigne', in B. Vincent, ed., *Les marginaux et les exclus dans l'histoire* (pp. 178–213), and David Moss, 'Bandits and Boundaries in Sardinia' (*Man*, N.S. 14, 1979, pp. 477–96). For the centrality of blood-vengeance in island banditry, Antonio Pigliaru, *La vendetta barbaricina come ordinamento giuridico* (Milan, 1975), and (for neighbouring CORSICA) Stephen Wilson, *Feuding, Conflict and Banditry in Nineteenth-Century Corsica* (Cambridge, 1988). The main innovation has been the extension of bandit studies from the south and the islands to central and even northern Italy, as in the studies collected in *Istituto 'Alcide Cervi' Annali*, 2/1, 1980, esp. part 2 (pp. 223–396), 'Brigantaggio, ribellione e devianza sociale nelle campagne dell'Italia centrale'. For north Italian regions, see various papers in G. Ortalli op. cit. Of special interest (not confined to its region) is the collection of studies in the folklore of law by, and ed., Luigi L. Lombardi Satriani and Mariano Meligrana, *Diritto egemone e diritto popolare: La Calabria negli studi di demologia giuridica* (Vibo Valentia, 1975).

For SPAIN, C. Bernaldo de Quirós, Luis Ardila, *El Bandolerismo Andaluz* (1933, repr. Madrid, 1978), gives the traditional facts of the quintessential bandit region, but the relevant parts of J. A. Pitt Rivers, *People of the Sierra* (Chicago, 1971) and J. Caro Baroja, *Ensayos sobre la Leteratura de Cordel* (Madrid, 1969) provides interpretations. Sophisticated and brief, Xavier Torres I Sans, *Els bandolers (s. XVI-XVII)* (Vic 1991) now supplements Joan Fuster, *El bandolerisme català* (Barcelona, 1962–3). Monographs on other Spanish regions are mentioned in the reference notes.

In BRITAIN, literature on Robin Hood continues to flourish. The most authoritative treatment is J. C. Holt, *Robin Hood* (London, 1982). Prof. Arfou Rees' work on Welsh outlaws and bandits remains unpublished. There is no literature of comparable interest on highwaymen. The most interesting work in FRANCE is also about the evolution of bandit legend and tradition, and is cited under that heading. The fullest work, *Mandrin* by F. Funck Brentano (Paris, 1908), is old and shows no insight. However, for the delinquency and its treatment in eighteenth-century Languedoc various works by Nicole Castan and Yves Castan are reliable and perceptive. Richard Cobb's writings on the Revolutionary period contain interesting sidelights. Bandit studies have flourished in GERMANY, stimulated by the controversial theses of Carsten Küther, *Räuber und Gauner in Deutschland: das organisierte Bandenwesen im 18. und frühen 19. Jahrhundert* (Göttingen, 1976). The major contribution is Uwe Danker, *Räuberbanden im Alten Reich um 1700: Ein Beitrag zur Geschichte von Herrschaft und Kriminalität in der Frühen Neuzeit* (Frankfurt, 2 vols, 1988). For an analysis of a famous gang in AUSTRIA, see Michael Pammer, 'Zur Johann Georg Grasslischen Räuber Complicität' (*Historicum*, Salzburg, 8/1988, pp. 29–33). Paul Hugger, *Sozialrebellen und Rechtsbrecher in der Schweiz* (Zurich, 1976) deals with the unexpected subject of possible social banditry in SWITZERLAND. Anton Blok, *De Bokkerijders: Roversbanden en geheime Genootschappen in de Landen van Overmaas [1730–1774]* (Amsterdam, 1991) is the fullest treatment of such bands for the NETHERLANDS.

EAST EUROPEAN banditry is discussed comparatively in Fikret Adanir op. cit. and Imre Rácz, *Couches militaires issues de la paysannerie libre en Europe orientale du quinzième au dix-septième siècles* (Debreczen, 1964). 'Dimensions de la Revolte Primitive en Europe Centrale et Orientale' (in the bulletin of the Groupe de Travail sur l'Europe Centrale et Orientale, Maison des Sciences de l'Homme, Paris: *Questions et Débats sur l'Europe Centrale et Orientale*, no. 4, Dec. 1985, pp. 85–135) is not on every bookshelf, but highly relevant for Greece, Romania and Armenia. On RUSSIA there seems to be little in other languages later than Denise Eeckhoute's 'Les brigands en Russie du dix-septième au dix-neuvième siècle' (*Revue d'Histoire Moderne et Contemporaine*, 2/1965, pp. 161–202). For BULGARIA, the old but valuable Georg Rosen, *Die Balkan-Haiduken* (Leipzig, 1878) and B. Tsvetkova, 'Mouvements anti-feodaux dans les terres bulgares' (*Etudes*

Historiques, Sofia, 1965). I have found A. V. Schweiger-Lerchenfeld, *Bosnien* (Vienna, 1878) helpful for the former YUGOSLAVIA, as also G. Castellan, *La vie quotidienne en Serbie au seuil de l'independance* (Paris, 1967). For GREECE, the main experts seem to be Dennis Skiotis, 'From bandit to Pasha: the first steps in the rise to power of Ali of Tepelen' (*Journal of Middle Eastern Studies*, 1971/2, pp. 219–44) and S. D. Asdrachas (cf. 'Quelques aspects du banditisme social en Grèce au XVIIIe siecle', *Etudes Balkaniques*, 1972/4, Sofia, pp. 97–112). I know of no study in a non-Slav language of Polish or Slovak banditry, but for CARPATHO-UKRAINE there is Ivan Olbracht's reportage, *Berge und Jahrhunderte* (East Berlin, 1952), the raw material for his wonderful novel (see below).

NORTH AMERICA has a large literature and an even larger body of film and fiction. I need only mention William Settle, *Jesse James Was His Name* (Columbia, MO, 1966), Stephen Tatum, *Inventing Billy the Kid: Visions of the Outlaw in America, 1881–1981* (Albuquerque, 1982) and Richard White, 'Outlaw Gangs of the Middle American Border: American Social Bandits' (*Western Historical Quarterly*, 12 Oct. 1981, pp. 387–408). James R. Green, *Grass-Roots Socialism: Radical Movements in the American Southwest 1895–1943* (Baton Rouge, 1978) is invaluable. Kent L. Steckmesser, 'Robin Hood and the American Outlaw' (*Journal of American Folklore*, 79, 1966, pp. 348–55) provides a basis for comparisons. Pat O'Malley, 'The Suppression of Banditry: Train Robbers in the US Border States and Bushrangers in Australia' (*Crime and Social Justice*, 16, Winter 1981, pp. 32–9) links the USA with AUSTRALIA on which see P. O'Malley, 'Class Conflict, Land and Social Banditry: Bushranging in Nineteenth-Century Australia' (*Social Problems*, 26, 1979, pp. 271–83). For his critique of Hobsbawm, see the Postscript. On the most famous Australian bandit, F. J. Mcquilton, *The*

Kelly Outbreak, 1878–1880: The Geographical Dimension of Social Banditry (Melbourne University Press, 1978), John H. Philips, *The Trial of Ned Kelly* (Sydney, 1987) and D. Morrissey, 'Ned Kelly's Sympathisers' (*Historical Studies* 18, 1978, University of Melbourne, pp. 228–96).

Good biographies of bandits today are usually written by historians (see the works cited above), though sometimes also by literary figures, notably Gavin Maxwell, *God Protect Me From My Friends* (London, 1957), a life of the Sicilian bandit Giuliano. Since the autobiographical statements by bandits are almost certain to come to us through the pens/keyboards of third parties, they must be treated with caution, as in the case of Panayot Hitov, the Bulgarian haiduk (in G. Rosen op. cit.) and even more of the south Italian brigand Crocco (in F. Cascella, *Il brigantaggio, ricerche sociologiche e antropologiche,* Aversa, 1907). E. Morsello S. de Sanctis, *Biografia di un bandito: Giuseppe Musolino di fronte alla psichiatria e alla sociologia. Studio medico-legale e considerazioni* (Milan, 1903) is another product of the same school of Italian criminology. The first-hand statements in the bibliography of Sardinian banditry and the Brazilian *cangaçeiros* must also be treated with care.

The scholarly study of the BANDIT TRADITION and the BANDIT LEGEND has made substantial advances. In addition to the works by Torres I Sans and Danker already cited, note the important introduction by Roger Chartier to *Figures de la gueuserie: Textes présentés par Roger Chartier* (Paris, 1982, esp. pp. 83–106), and Dominique Blanc-Daniel Fabre, *Le Brigand de Cavanac: le fait divers, le roman, l'histoire* (Editions Verdier, Lagrasse, 1982). Linda Lewin, 'Oral Tradition and Elite Myth: The Legend of Antônio Silvino in Brazilian Popular Culture' (*Journal of Latin American Lore*, 5:2, 1979, pp. 157–204), is an outstanding example of such a study. For the ballads and verses themselves, R. Daus, *Der epische Zyklus der*

Cangaçeiros in der Volkspoesie Nordostbrasiliens (Berlin, 1969). For Spain, Julio Caro Baroja, op. cit., A. Dozon, *Chansons populaires bulgares inédites* (Paris, 1875) and Adolf Strausz, *Bulgarische Volksdichtung* (Vienna/Leipzig, 1895) give a reasonable selection of haiduk ballads. What linguistic ignorance debars most of us from is indicated by the English summary of J. Horak and K. Plicka, *Zbojnicke piesne sloveskoho l'udu* (Bratislava, 1963) which contains 700 songs about bandits, all from Slovakia.

Among the numerous bandit novels, by far the best I know is Ivan Olbracht, *Der Räuber Nikola Schuhaj* (East Berlin, 1953). *Mehmed My Hawk* by Yashar Kemal (London, 1961) – another Communist literary figure – is excellent. The classic bandit novel, of course, is the Chinese *Shuihu Zhuan* (in the modern transliteration), translated by Pearl Buck as *All Men Are Brothers* (New York, 1937). E. About's *Le roi des montagnes* is a disenchanted picture of post-liberation Greek brigandage. Walter Scott's *Rob Roy* (with a useful historical introduction) is much less misleading about its subject than the same author's *Ivanhoe* is about Robin Hood.

Bandits have been the subject of numerous films, TV programmes and videos. None of these is of value as a historical source, but at least two add greatly to our understanding of the bandit environment: V. de Seta's *Banditi ad Orgosolo* and Francesco Rosi's masterly *Salvatore Giuliano*.

Index

***